Financial Globalization

FINANCIAL GLOBALIZATION

JASON H. CARDWELL
EDITOR

Nova Science Publishers, Inc.
New York

For permission to use material from this book please contact us:
Telephone 631-231-7269; Fax 631-231-8175
Web Site: http://www.novapublishers.com

LIBRARY OF CONGRESS CATALOGING-IN-PUBLICATION DATA

Financial globalization / editor, Jason H. Cardwell.
p. cm.
Includes index.
ISBN 978-1-60692-190-6 (softcover)
1. International finance. 2. Globalization--Economic aspects. I. Cardwell, Jason H.
HG3881.F5186 2009
332'.042--dc22
2009051580

Published by Nova Science Publishers, Inc. † New York

CONTENTS

PREFACE

Financial globalization refers to the ongoing integration of once poorly connected national financial markets. A key aspect of globalization is a decline in financial home bias— the tendency for domestic saving to be invested predominantly at home, with domestic portfolios tilted heavily toward home-country assets. Recent years have in fact seen a pronounced decline in home bias, with a record fraction of global saving going to cross-border investments. Indeed, in 2005 and 2006, the share of global saving invested abroad climbed past 50 percent for the first time. The trend toward greater cross-border investment has been worldwide, with the United States, other advanced economies, and emerging economies all investing a markedly higher fraction of saving abroad. Significantly, U.S. external investment as a share of saving has risen less dramatically than the share for other countries. Comparing the mid-1990s with the middle of the current decade, we see that U.S. outflows as a share of domestic saving have risen by roughly 20 percentage points; the increase abroad has been close to 35 percentage points. As a result, the United States now lags the rest of the world by a considerable margin in the share of national saving invested abroad. It is instructive to consider the smaller scale of outflows from the United States in light of the current account balance of payments accounting identity described earlier. In particular, had outflows from the United States risen in line with the global trend, the country would have required that much more inward investment to finance an unchanged sequence of current account deficits. In turn, more robust U.S. demand for foreign assets, and the consequent need to attract additional inflows, would have placed downward pressure on the dollar, leading to at least somewhat smaller deficits. This scenario illustrates a more general point: developments that lead to shifts in gross capital flows have important feedback effects on net flows.

Chapter 1 - This paper analyzes the potential effect of global market competition on inflation dynamics. It does so through the lens of the Calvo model of staggered price setting, which implies that inflation depends on expected future inflation and a measure of marginal costs. I modify the assumption of a constant elasticity of demand, standard in this model, to provide a channel through which an increase in the number of traded goods may affect the degree of strategic complementarity in price setting and hence alter the dynamic response of inflation to marginal costs. I first discuss the behavior of the variables that drive the impact of trade openness on this response, and then I evaluate whether an increase in the variety of traded goods of the magnitude observed in the United States in the 1990s might have a significant quantitative impact. I find that it is difficult to argue that such an increase in trade would have generated a sufficiently large increase in U.S. market competition to reduce the slope of the inflation-marginal cost relation.

Chapter 2 - Despite heavy borrowing in recent years, the United States has financed its large current account deficits without experiencing an unusual buildup in foreign investors' holdings of U.S. assets. A new analysis suggests that this somewhat surprising development is attributable largely to rapid financial globalization, with cross-border flows worldwide rising as fast as flows into the United States. However, it could be harder for the country to sustain large deficits on favorable terms if the current wave of globalization subsided or the rate at which U.S. investors buy foreign assets increased.

Chapter 3 features testimony before the U. S. House of Representatives.

In: Financial Globalization
Editor: Jason H. Cardwell

ISBN: 978-1-60692-190-6

Chapter 1

GLOBALIZATION AND INFLATION DYNAMICS: THE IMPACT OF INCREASED COMPETITION*

Argia M. Sbordone

ABSTRACT

This paper analyzes the potential effect of global market competition on inflation dynamics. It does so through the lens of the Calvo model of staggered price setting, which implies that inflation depends on expected future inflation and a measure of marginal costs. I modify the assumption of a constant elasticity of demand, standard in this model, to provide a channel through which an increase in the number of traded goods may affect the degree of strategic complementarity in price setting and hence alter the dynamic response of inflation to marginal costs. I first discuss the behavior of the variables that drive the impact of trade openness on this response, and then I evaluate whether an increase in the variety of traded goods of the magnitude observed in the United States in the 1990s might have a significant quantitative impact. I find that it is difficult to argue that such an increase in trade would have generated a sufficiently large increase in U.S. market competition to reduce the slope of the inflation-marginal cost relation.

Keywords: inflation dynamics, globalization

---

* This is an edited, reformatted and augmented version of a Federal Reserve Bank of New York publication dated April 2008.

1. Introduction

The policy debate about the macroeconomic effects of globalization has centered on two main themes: that globalization has contributed to bring down US inflation, and that it has affected the sensitivity of inflation to output fluctuations. Several recent policymakers speeches have addressed the issue of whether more intense competition, generated by the increase in trade experienced since the '90s, has changed the role of domestic factors in shaping the inflation process. Chairman Bernanke (2007), for example, has underlined how the dependence of factor markets from economic conditions abroad might have reduced the market power of domestic sellers, how the pricing power of domestic producers might have declined, and how lower import prices both of final and intermediate goods might have contributed to maintain overall inflation at low levels. Similarly, President Yellen (2006) and Governor Kohn (2006) have discussed several direct and indirect impacts of more global markets on US inflation.

In this paper I explore how globalization might have impacted US inflation by using the new Keynesian model of inflation dynamics as analytical framework. Within this framework, I focus in particular on the effects that an increase in market competition generated by an increase in trade might have on the sensitivity of inflation to real marginal costs of production.

The relationship between inflation and marginal cost is a key determinant of the overall 'slope' of the new Keynesian Phillips curve (NKPC), which links the dynamics of inflation to the level of economic activity. In the price setting model most often used to derive the NKPC (the one based on the contribution by Calvo, 1983), this relationship depends primarily on the frequency of price changes, but it is also affected by strategic complementarity in price setting. It is this last mechanism that provides a way of formalizing the 'globalization' argument, according to which the increase in the openness of the economy has affected the sensitivity of inflation to output variations.

I depart here from the assumption of constant elasticity of substitution among differentiated goods, which is typically made in the Calvo model, and adopt a specification where the elasticity is a function of the firm's relative share of the market. This implies that changes in the importance of trade that affect relative market shares affect in turn the elasticity of demand faced by firms, and hence their desired mark-ups, and so ultimately may have an impact on the elasticity of aggregate inflation to real marginal costs and the slope of the Phillips curve.

To preview the results: I find that an increase in the number of goods traded is able to generate the sort of real rigidities that may lead to a change in the slope of the Phillips curve. The sign of the change, however, depends on how fast the elasticity of substitution among goods increases, and different parametrizations of the demand function may lead to different answers. For large enough increases in the number of goods traded, the slope of the Phillips curve is in general declining: however, the evidence on trade patterns so far provides little ground to assume that we are yet in the declining portion of the curve.

There are a number of caveats to these results. In particular, the elasticity of inflation to marginal cost is only one of the determinants of the slope of the Phillips curve - the overall response of inflation to output (or output gap) - and its increase or decline does not necessarily imply that the latter is of the same sign. However, this is arguably the component that is affected the most by variations in the degree of market competition and it is the one relied upon in discussions of the effects of global competition on the "pricing power" of domestic firms; hence it is the one where a study of these variations should be centered. I return to this point in the conclusion.

The paper is organized as follows. Section 2 overviews existing evidence about the change in the slope of the Phillips curve and discusses the ensued debate. Section 3 analyzes the channels through which the increased trade that characterizes globalization may affect the dynamics of inflation. Section 4 introduces the analytical framework that is used to pin down these effects, and section 5 adapts the framework to analyze the effects of firms' entry on the dynamics of price adjustments. Sections 6 and 7 evaluate the quantitative impact of trade increase on the marginal cost slope of the Phillips curve, and section 8 concludes.

2. Has the Slope of the Phillips Curve Changed?

The policymakers' concerns over a change in the slope of the Phillips curve in recent years derive from its role in assessing the cost of disinflation. A flatter Phillips curve carries the implication that, for a given degree of inflation persistence, reducing inflation involves a higher 'sacrifice ratio' than otherwise, namely it requires enduring a longer period of unemployment above the natural rate for every desired percentage point of reduction in inflation. On the other hand, as noted by Mishkin (2007), a flatter Phillips curve also implies that an overheated economy will tend to generate a smaller increase in inflation.

Most of the empirical analyses supporting the policymakers' concerns address the issue of the flattening of the Phillips curve in the context of traditional 'accelerationists' Phillips curves. Roberts (2006) and Williams (2006), for example, estimate smaller Phillips curves' slopes in samples covering the post-84 period. Williams in particular analyzes samples with moving starting points - from 1980:1 to 1999:4, but with a fix end point (2006:4) and finds evidence of a flatter curve and a higher sacrifice ratio in the samples that start in the 1990s relative to those estimated in the full sample. However, he also finds that in the more recent samples the unit sum restriction on the lag coefficients, which defines the accelerationist curve, is violated. Furthermore, when in these samples the lag coefficients are left unconstrained, the estimates of the slope coefficient indeed increases.

An alternative source of evidence that the slope of the Phillips curve has declined in more recent samples is provided by estimates in the context of general equilibrium models. Boivin and Giannoni (2006), for example, estimate that the coefficient of marginal cost in a new Keynesian Phillips curve (NKPC) declines from .011 to .008 in the post '84 period; Smets and Wouters (2007) in a similar general equilibrium model report that the estimated interval between price changes is higher in the 1984-2004 sample relative to the 1966-1979 period, which imply that the slope declined in the more recent period.

While the just cited studies aim at relating the change in the inflation-output trade-off to the change in monetary policy that took place in the early '80s, in a recent BIS study Borio and Filardo (2007) link instead variations in the slope of the Phillips curve to globalization. Specifically, they estimate a traditional Phillips curve for many countries over the two periods 1980-1992 and 1993-2005, and document that in the more recent period there has been both a decline in the autoregressive coefficient - hence a decline in inflation persistence, and a decline in the slope, hence a drop in the sensitivity of inflation to domestic output gap. For the United States, in particular, the authors report a decline in the estimated coefficient of lagged inflation from .92 to .82 across the two samples, and a decline in the elasticity of inflation to output gap from .13 to .09. They take this evidence as the starting point of the investigation of a 'global slack' hypothesis, according to which the decline in the sensitivity of inflation to domestic measures of output gap is explained by the fact that global measures of demand pressure have become in the later period the main driving force of inflation dynamics.

A successor study (Ihrig et al. 2007) finds that the purported support for the global slack hypothesis is not robust to the specification of the measures of global slack. For example, the study finds that variables such as domestic output time the ratio of trade to GDP, and import prices time the ratio of imports to GDP do not have statistically significant coefficients. The study, however, does not dispute the evidence that the Phillips curve appears to have flattened since the '90s; it contests the interpretation that this is indeed an effect of globalization. Overall, the authors in fact conclude that the estimated effect of foreign output gaps is in general insignificant, that there is no evidence that the trend decline in the sensitivity of inflation to domestic output is due to globalization, nor they find increased sensitivity of inflation to import prices.

An IMF study (2006) also estimates traditional inflation regressions where the coefficient on the slack variable interacts with measures of central bank credibility and openness of the economy. The study estimates a negative coefficient on the interaction term between domestic output gap and trade openness, measured by the share of non-oil imports in GDP, and interprets this result as evidence that the increase in trade has contributed to the decline of the slope of the Phillips curve. The study, however, examines the group of advanced economies as a whole, and doesn't present results for the US alone. Finally, in the context of a similar traditional Phillips curve estimated for the U.S., Ball (2006) allows interaction of the output coefficient with trade, and finds only a modest effect.

In this paper I do not estimate the slope of the Phillips curve, but propose instead a way to analyze the quantitative importance of globalization effects on such a slope. Specifically I lay down the channels through which an increase in market competition can generate a flattening of the Phillips curve, in the context of the new Keynesian model of inflation dynamics.

3. Channels of Globalization Effects on Inflation

The basic channel emphasized both in policy debates and empirical studies as potential carrier of globalization effects on inflation dynamics is trade integration, which especially when accompanied by policy incentives, is argued to bolster competition. Increased competition, the argument goes, creates two effects: a direct effect of containment of costs, by restraining increases in workers' compensations and reducing real import prices, and a second, indirect effect of creating pressure to innovate, which contributes to increasing productivity. Higher productivity in turn further lowers production costs: if markups are constant, lower production costs reduce the pressure on prices. But the margins that firms are willing to charge over their costs might be reduced as well, moderating the extent of price increases.

To understand how these effects work, it is useful to decompose the relation between consumer price inflation and domestic output, the one typically analyzed in empirical studies, in three distinct parts. First, there is the relation between CPI inflation and domestic inflation. In an open economy, consumer price inflation reflects the price dynamics of goods produced both domestically and abroad that are consumed at home. Secondly, there is the relation between domestic inflation and the marginal cost of production, and finally the relationship between the marginal cost of production and domestic output.

The central relationship, that describes how variations in marginal cost translate into fluctuations in domestic prices, is the one most likely affected by an increase in competition.

When analyzed through the lenses of the new Keynesian approach to the construction of a Phillips curve, the strength of this relationship depends on a number of factors. The first is the frequency of price revisions: the longer prices are kept fixed, the more nominal disturbances translate into real effects, rather than aggregate inflation. This is referred to as the nominal rigidity component. The second component is the sensitivity of the desired firms' price to marginal costs versus other prices. If price setters take into account other firms' prices when they set their own price, then the presence of even a small number of firms that do not change their price induces flexible-price firms to change their price by a lesser amount. A third component is the sensitivity of marginal costs to the own output of the firm (versus its sensitivity to the average marginal cost): when marginal costs of the price setter are increasing in its own output, the desired price increase is smaller because the firm takes into account the decline in marginal cost due to the loss in demand when the price is increased. Finally, the pricing decisions are affected by the sensitivity of the firm's own output to its relative price, namely by how elastic is the demand curve of the individual producer. The last three components are commonly referred to as 'strategic complementarity' or 'real rigidity' channels.[1]

Both nominal and real rigidities are known to be important in assessing the size of the 'slope' of the new Keynesian Phillips curve with respect to marginal costs. They have been analyzed in theoretical works and explored in empirical studies aiming at reconciling estimated 'slopes' with reasonable degrees of nominal rigidity.[2]

In this paper I focus on the real rigidity component and analyze how it can be affected by the openness of the economy, through the increase in competitiveness generated by an increase in the number of goods traded in the economy.

To do this I borrow from the new trade literature, and in particular from a recent contribution by Melitz and Ott aviano (2005), who present a model of trade with monopolistic competition and firm heterogeneity to study the effect of trade liberalization on productivity and mark-ups. The authors show that import competition induces a downward shift in the distribution of markups across firms. A key element of their model is the dependence of the elasticity of demand upon the relative size of the market. This setting has been used in a macro general equilibrium model by Bilbiie et al (2006a and 2006b) to study endogenous entry as a propagation of business cycles, and the efficiency properties of the model, adopting a framework of flexible prices.

Here I study instead a model of staggered prices. I consider a monopolistically competitive market where there is a fixed entry cost, and a given distribution of firms. A reduction in the individual firms production costs moves up the firms' distribution curve, making profitable for more firms to enter the market. The resulting increase in the variety of goods traded increases the overall degree of competition: this is captured in the model by making the demand elasticity, and hence the mark-up, vary with the number of goods that are traded. Variable mark-ups in turn impact the price setting process and the dynamics of the relationship between inflation and marginal cost.

My focus is specifically on how the process of new entries and the interaction of firms in the price setting process affect the relationship between aggregate inflation and marginal costs. I will not discuss the other two components of the CPI inflation - domestic output relationship that I described, the relation between domestic and CPI inflation, and the relation between marginal cost and domestic output. These relationships obviously matter for the assessment of the overall effect of openness on the Phillips curve's slope, and an explicit modeling of the Phillips curve in open economy may as well illustrate that its slope is lower than that of the closed economy.[3] Nevertheless, understanding the channels through which market entry changes the degree of real rigidity, and how that may emphasize or reduce the inflation-output trade-off, is of primary importance.

Similarly, I will not discuss effects of globalization on inflation of the kind argued by Rogoff (2003, 2006), that in a global environment central banks have less incentive to inflate the economy. Although this lower incentive is another effect of the increased competitiveness of the economy, it is related to central banks' incentives,[4] rather than to the market mechanisms to which I am interested in here.

4. A Structural Framework

The Calvo model of staggered prices provides a useful framework to disentangle the various theoretical channels that compose the inflation-marginal cost relationship. Since the baseline model is well known, here I summarize its main features to set the stage for the generalizations that I discuss next.

The model has a continuum of monopolistic firms, indexed by i, which produce differentiated goods, also indexed by i, over which consumers' preferences are defined. Firms produce with a constant returns to scale technology and have access to economy-wide factor markets. The optimal consumption allocation determines the demand for each differentiated good $ct(i)$ as

$$c_t(i) = C_t \left(\frac{p_t(i)}{P_t} \right)^{-\theta} \tag{1}$$

for $\theta > 1$; here $p_t(i)$ is the individual good i price, C_t indicates firm level output, defined by the constant-elasticity-of substitution aggregator of Dixit and Stiglitz:

$$C_t = \left[\int c_t(i)^{(\theta-1)/\theta} di \right]^{\theta/(\theta-1)}, \tag{2}$$

and P_t is the corresponding aggregate price (the minimum cost to buy a unit of the aggregate good C_t): $P_t = \left[\int p_t(i)^{1-\theta} di\right]^{1/(1-\theta)}$. The model further assumes random intervals between price changes: in every period, only a fraction $(1 - \alpha)$ of the firms can set a new price, independently of the past history of price changes, which will then be kept fixed until the next time the firm is drawn to change prices again. By letting α vary between 0 and 1, the model nests assumptions about the degree of price stickiness from perfect flexibility ($\alpha = 0$) to complete price rigidity (the limit as $\alpha \rightarrow 1$). The expected time between price changes is then $1/(1 - \alpha)$.

The pricing problem of a firm that revises its price in period t is to choose the price pt (i) that maximizes its expected stream of profits

$$E_t \left\{ \Sigma_{j=0}^{\infty} Q_{t,t+j} \mathrm{P}_{t+j}(i) \right\}, \tag{3}$$

where time t profits $P_t(i)$ are a function $P(p_t(i), P_t, y_t(i), Y_t; \Gamma_t)$; $y_t(i)$ is firm's output, defined by (1), $Q_{t,t+j}$ is a stochastic discount factor, and the variable Γ_t stands for all other aggregate variables. The first order condition for the optimal price is

$$E_t \left\{ \Sigma_{j=0}^{\infty} Q_{t,t+j} \mathsf{P}_1 \left(p_t^*, P_{t+j}, y_{t+j}\left(i\right), Y_{t+j}; \Gamma_{t+j} \right) \right\} = 0, \tag{4}$$

where the evolution of aggregate prices is

$$P_t = \left[(1-\alpha) p_t^{*1-\theta} + \alpha P_{t-1}^{1-\theta} \right]^{\frac{1}{1-\theta}}. \tag{5}$$

Log-linearizing these two equilibrium conditions around a steady state with zero inflation, with usual manipulations, one obtains the familiar form of inflation dynamics as function of expected inflation and real marginal costs s_t

$$\pi_t = \zeta \widehat{s}_t + \beta E_t \pi_{t+1} \tag{6}$$

where a hat indicates the log-deviation from a non-stochastic steady state, β is the steady state value of the discount factor, and the 'slope' is defined as[5]

$$\zeta = \frac{(1-\alpha\beta)(1-\alpha)}{\alpha} \tag{7}$$

In this baseline framework, the extent of the nominal rigidity determines how marginal costs translate into inflation fluctuations. In order to consider other potential channels of the kind discussed above the model needs to be generalized. where II denotes the gross trend inflation rate. The slope in this case depends not only upon the primitives of the Calvo model, the probability of changing prices 1-a and the elasticity

4.1. The Inflation/Marginal Cost Relation: Some Generalizations

Generalizations of the baseline model can lead to changes in the nominal rigidity component of the slope or introduce some form of real rigidity of the kind discussed previously by adding new terms to expression (7).

One instance in which the nominal rigidity term is modified, despite maintaining an exogenous probability of changing prices, occurs when one allows for a non-zero steady state inflation. In this case the expression for inflation dynamics is derived as a (log) linear approximation of the model equilibrium conditions (4) and (5) around a steady state characterized by positive, rather than zero inflation, as it is the case in the baseline model. Such an approximation modifies the terms in the discount and the rigidity coefficient in the slope (9). As first shown by Ascari (2004), in such a case the slope coefficient would be:

$$\zeta = \frac{\left(1 - \alpha\beta\overline{\Pi}^{\theta}\right)\left(1 - \alpha\overline{\Pi}^{\theta-1}\right)}{\alpha\overline{\Pi}^{\theta-1}}, \tag{8}$$

where $\overline{\Pi}$ denotes the gross trend inflation rate. The slope in this case depends not only upon the primitives of the Calvo model, the probability of changing prices 1 - α and the elasticity of demand, but also upon the steady state level of inflation. In this case the *NKPC* has also a richer dynamics, because it includes additional forward-looking terms, unless particular forms of indexation are postulated.[6]

A further modification of the nominal rigidity component is obtained by replacing the assumption of a constant probability of price re-optimization with a state-dependent probability (see Dotsey, King and Wolman 1999).

The generalizations that provide a more direct channel through which the competitive effect of more global markets integration can alter the Phillips curve's slope are those that introduce real rigidity factors in the slope coefficient. Such modifications were at first introduced with the purpose of reconciling empirical estimates of the slope with a degree of nominal rigidity more in line with that documented in firms' surveys.[7] In fact, for any given degree of nominal rigidity, the existence of strategic complementarity lowers the slope or, alternatively, a given empirical estimate of the slope is consistent with a lower degree of nominal rigidity.

Assuming for example that some or all factor markets are firm-specific implies that the marginal cost of supplying goods to the market is not equal for all goods at any specific point in time. In such cases firms' marginal costs depend not only on economy-wide factors, but also on the firm's own output[8] and, for any given increase in marginal cost, this dependence makes the desired price increase smaller. Returning to a baseline case with zero steady state inflation, the slope ζ in these cases becomes

$$\zeta = \frac{(1-\alpha\beta)(1-\alpha)}{\alpha}\frac{1}{1+\theta s_y}, \tag{9}$$

where the strategic complementarity term $\frac{1}{1+\theta s_y}$ depends upon the demand elasticity θ, which measures the sensitivity of the own output of the firm to its relative price, and the sensitivity of the firm's marginal cost to its own output, s_y. The parameter s_y in turn depends on other model assumptions: for example, when labor is traded in an economy-wide labor market but capital is firm specific and therefore cannot be instantaneously reallocated across firms, a constant returns to scale production function implies that s_y is equal to the ratio of the output elasticities with respect to capital and labor.[9] In a more general case where labor markets as well are firm-specific, the parameter s_y is a composite parameter that includes also the elasticity of the marginal disutility of work with respect to output increases (Woodford, 2003).

Another extension is the case in which each firm's desired mark-up over its marginal cost depends upon the prices of other firms. Since the desired mark-up depends on the firm's elasticity of demand, a variable desired mark-up requires a variable demand elasticity. Modeling this case then requires departing from the constant elasticity of substitution assumption of the Dixit-Stiglitz aggregator. For example, the aggregator proposed in the macro literature by Kimball (1995) allows for the elasticity of substitution between differentiated goods to be a function of their relative market share.

Kimball was interested in a variable elasticity of demand to generate countercyclical movements in the firm's desired mark-up, and sufficient real rigidity to make a model of sticky prices plausible (i.e. without having to assume too large a percentage of firms with long periods of unadjusted prices). His objective was to generate more flexible demand functions, particularly 'quasi-kinked' demand functions, characterized by the property that for the firm at its normal market share it is easier to lose customers by increasing its relative price than to gain customers by lowering its relative price. By making the elasticity of demand depend upon the firm's relative sales, Kimball's preferences generate another kind of strategic complementarity that amplifies the effect of nominal disturbances and, everything else equal, reduces the size of the Phillips curve's slope.[10] Such property has spurred new research on various implications of the assumption of a non-constant elasticity of substitution. Dotsey and King (2005) use a specific functional form for the Kimball aggregator in a calibrated DSGE model to study the dynamic response of inflation and output to monetary shocks in the context of a state-dependent pricing model. Levin, Lopez-Salido and Yun

(2006) adopt the Kimball specification to analyze the interaction of strategic complementarity and steady state inflation. In empirical work, Eichenbaum and Fisher (2007) use the same specification to pin down a realistic estimate of the frequency of price re-optimization in the Calvo model. Finally, in the context of an open economy model, Gust et al. (2006) extend these preferences to the demand of home produced and imported goods, to show that with strategic complementarity lower trade costs reduce the pass-through of exchange rate movements to import prices.

Departing from the constant demand elasticity assumption along the lines of Kimball, the consumption aggregate in (2) is replaced by an aggregate C_t implicitly defined by

$$\int_{\Omega} \psi\left(\frac{c_t(i)}{C_t}\right) di = 1, \tag{10}$$

where ψ (.) is an increasing, strictly concave function, and Ω is the set of all potential goods produced (a real line). With this notation the Dixit-Stiglitz aggregator corresponds to the case where $\psi\left(c_t(i)/C_t\right) = \left(c_t(i)/C_t\right)^{(\theta-1)/\theta}$ for some $\theta > 1$. With an aggregator function of the form (10) one can show[11] that the Calvo model implies an inflation dynamics of the baseline form, where the slope (again for simplicity, in the case of zero steady state inflation) becomes

Here $\bar{\theta}$ is the steady state value of the firm's elasticity of demand, which is now a function θ (x) of the firm's relative sales (denoted by x); $\bar{\epsilon}_{\mu}$ is the steady state value of the function ~ μ (x) that represents the elasticity of the mark-up function μ (x), which also depends on the firm's relative sales; $\bar{s}_y$ is the steady state value of the elasticity of the firm's marginal cost with respect to its own sales. The interactions of the new variables in the strategic complementarity term[1] $\frac{1}{1+\bar{\theta}(\bar{s}_y+\bar{\epsilon}_{\mu})}$ determines to what extent the slope ζ differs from that of the baseline case.

Expression (11) formalizes all the channels discussed in section 3 as those through which globalization may affect the strength of the relationship between inflation and marginal costs. It shows that the slope coefficient depends upon a number of variables: (i) the frequency of price revisions, represented by the coefficient α : less frequent price revisions (a higher value of α) correspond to lower ζ; (ii) the sensitivity of the desired firm's price to marginal cost versus other prices, the term $\overline{\epsilon}_{\mu}$: higher sensitivity reduces the slope; (iii) the sensitivity of marginal cost to the own output of the firm, the term $\overline{s}_y$; and (iv) the sensitivity of the firm's own output to the relative price, $\overline{\theta}$. In addition, the slope is possibly affected by the level of steady state inflation, which may interact with the demand elasticity, as in (8).

The Calvo model enriched with these modifications is now a suitable framework for discussing the effects of globalization: the task is to relate the factors that drive the value of the slope to the increase in trade openness, that is one of the characteristics of a more global environment. This is what I consider next. Leaving aside the issue of whether globalization affects the frequency of price adjustments, and more generally the nominal rigidity term, in the next section I focus on the effects of an increase in trade on the strategic complementarity term.

5. The Effect of Firms' Entry

5.1. Kimball Preferences with a Variable Number of Goods

I extend Kimball's (1995) model to an environment where the number of traded goods is variable. The model implies that the elasticity of demand depends on the firm's relative output share: by relating this share to the number of goods traded the steady-state elasticity of demand becomes function of the number of traded goods in steady state. This implies that the degree of strategic complementarity varies with the number of traded goods, hence so does the slope of the inflation-marginal cost curve.

I assume that households' utility is defined over an aggregate C_t of differentiated goods c_t (i), defined implicitly by (10), where ψ (.) is an increasing, strictly concave function, and I also assume that ψ (0) = 0. If the set of goods that happen to be sold is [0, N] , then ct (i) = 0 for all i > N, and Ct satisfies[12]

$$\int_0^N \psi\left(\frac{c_t(i)}{C_t}\right) di = 1. \qquad (12)$$

The elasticity of demand, in this set-up, is defined as a function

$$\theta(x) = -\frac{\psi'(x)}{x\psi''(x)}, \tag{13}$$

where x indicates the relative market share of the differentiated goods. In Kimball's formulation the elasticity of demand is lower for those goods that sell more because their relative price is lower. Accordingly, the desired mark-up pricing over costs is as well a function of the market share:

$$\mu(x) = \frac{\theta(x)}{\theta(x) - 1}. \tag{14}$$

The optimal consumption allocation across goods is the solution to the following problem

$$\min_{\{c_t(i)\}} \int_0^N p_t(i)\, c_t(i)\, di \qquad \text{s.t.} \qquad \int_0^N \psi\left(\frac{c_t(i)}{C_t}\right) di = 1$$

The first order conditions for this problem are

$$p_t(i) = \frac{1}{\Lambda_t C_t}\psi'\left(\frac{c_t(i)}{C_t}\right) \tag{15}$$

for each $i \in [0, N]$, where Λ_t is the Lagrange multiplier for constraint (12). The solution to this minimization problem gives the demand for each good i as

$$c_t(i) = C_t \psi'^{-1}\left(p_t(i)\, \Lambda_t C_t\right), \tag{16}$$

where Λ_t is implicitly defined by the requirement that

$$\int_0^N \psi\left(\psi'^{-1}\left(p_t(i)\, \Lambda_t C_t\right)\right) di = 1. \tag{17}$$

Expression (17) defines a price index $\widetilde{P}_t \equiv \frac{1}{\Lambda_t C_t}$ for any set of prices $\{pt\ (i)\}$, which is independent of C_t. We can then write the demand curve for good i as

$$y_t(i) = Y_t \psi'^{-1}\left(\frac{p_t(i)}{\widetilde{P}_t}\right) \tag{18}$$

Note that the aggregate 'price' $\widetilde{P}_t$ is not in general the same as the conventional price index, which here is defined, as in the case of Dixit-Stiglitz preferences, as the cost of a unit of the composite good, that is

$$P_t = \frac{1}{C_t}\int_0^N p_t(i)\, c_t(i)\, di = \int_0^N p_t(i)\, \psi'^{-1}\left(\frac{p_t(i)}{\widetilde{P}_t}\right) di, \tag{19}$$

where the second equality follows from (18). Both Pt and ^{e}Pt, however, are homogeneous of degree one functions in $\{p_t\ (i)\ \}$.

5.2. Steady State with Symmetric Prices

I am interested in the properties of the demand curve in a steady state with symmetric prices $pt\ (i) = pt$ for all i. In this case it follows from (12) that the relative demand $c_t\ (i)\ /C_t$ is equal to

$$c_t(i)\,/C_t = \psi^{-1}\left(\frac{1}{N}\right) \tag{20}$$

for all i, and from (15):

$$\widetilde{P}_t = \frac{p_t}{\psi'\left(\psi^{-1}\left(\frac{1}{N}\right)\right)}. \tag{21}$$

From the definition of P_t in (19) it also follows that

$$P_t = p_t \left[N\psi^{-1}\left(\frac{1}{N}\right)\right]. \tag{22}$$

The elasticity of demand in such a steady state, denoted by $\overline{\theta}$, is

$$\overline{\theta} = -\frac{\psi'(x)}{x\psi''(x)}, \tag{23}$$

where $x = \psi^{-1}\left(\frac{1}{N}\right)$ denotes the relative share in the symmetric steady state. Note how this elasticity differs from the case of the Dixit-Stiglitz aggregator, where the elasticity of demand is a constant $\theta(x) = \theta$ for all x. Here the demand elasticity depends upon the relative market share of the good, and its value in steady state, $\overline{\theta}$, is a function of the number of goods traded in steady state, N. I am interested in seeing how this steady state elasticity $\overline{\theta}$ varies with N. The extent of this variation depends on how the elasticity function $\theta(x)$ varies with x[13].

The assumptions made so far do not have implications for the sign of θ' (x). However, if we assume, as Kimball (1995) does, that the function $\theta(x)$ is decreasing in x, then, since $\psi^{-1}\left(\frac{1}{N}\right)$ is decreasing in N, it follows that $\overline{\theta}$ is increasing in N. This is in line with the general intuition that more goods are traded in a market, more likely it is for the demand to decrease more in response to a small increase in prices.

As $\overline{\theta}$ varies with the number of goods traded, so does the desired mark-up of prices over costs, evaluated in steady state. I define the steady state desired mark-up as $\overline{\mu} \equiv \frac{\overline{\theta}}{\overline{\theta}-1}$ if θ is increasing in N, then the steady state desired mark-up is decreasing in N. For what it is discussed later on it is also important to evaluate the extent to which the mark-up itself, as defined in (14), varies with the relative sales, and therefore with the number of traded goods.

The elasticity of the mark-up function is defined as

$$\epsilon_{\mu}(x) = \frac{\partial \log \mu(x)}{\partial \log x} = \frac{x\mu'(x)}{\mu(x)} \tag{24}$$

which, evaluated at $x = \psi^{-1}\left(\frac{1}{N}\right)$, is donated as[14]

$$\bar{\epsilon}_{\mu} = \frac{x\mu'(x)}{\mu(x)}. \tag{25}$$

The elasticity $\bar{\epsilon}_{\mu}$ determines how much $\bar{\mu}$ varies for a small variation in N.[15] Since

$$\frac{\partial \log \mu}{\partial \log N} = \frac{\partial \log \mu}{\partial \log x} \cdot \frac{\partial \log x}{\partial \log N} = \bar{\epsilon}_{\mu} \cdot \frac{\partial \log x}{\partial \log N}$$

and since $\frac{1}{N} = \psi(x)$,

$$\frac{\partial \log N}{\partial \log x} = -\frac{x\psi'(x)}{\psi(x)} = -N\psi^{-1}\left(\frac{1}{N}\right)\psi'\left(\psi^{-1}\left(\frac{1}{N}\right)\right),$$

we have that

$$\frac{\partial \log \mu}{\partial \log N} = \frac{-\bar{\epsilon}_{\mu}}{N\psi^{-1}\left(\frac{1}{N}\right)\psi'\left(\psi^{-1}\left(\frac{1}{N}\right)\right)}.$$

The elasticity of μ with respect to N has therefore the opposite sign of the elasticity $\bar{\epsilon}_{\mu}$. In turn we can determine how $\epsilon_{\mu}(x)$ must vary with N by considering how $\epsilon_{\mu}(x)$ varies with x. Since we can argue that log μ is a convex function of log x,[16] it follows from definition (24) that $\epsilon_{\mu}(x)$ is an increasing function of x: we can then conclude that $\bar{\epsilon}_{\mu}$ is a decreasing function of N.

Finally, it can be shown that the steady state sensitivity of the firm's marginal cost to its own output, $\bar{s}_y$, is also a function of N. This elasticity depends upon assumptions about the form of the production function and about consumer preferences, which I haven't spelled out yet. I make here some simplifying assumptions to illustrate the nature of the dependence of $\overline{s}_y$ on N. Let the production function of firm i be

$$y_t(i) = h_t(i)^{1-a} - \Phi \tag{26}$$

where Φ is a fixed cost. This leads to a labor demand function

$$h_t(i) = (y_t(i) + \Phi)^{\frac{1}{1-a}} \tag{27}$$

Assuming an economy -wide labor market, with nominal wage W_t, the total cost of production of firm i is $W_t h_t$ (i) , and its real marginal cost is

$$s_t(i) = \frac{MC_t}{P_t}(y_t(i);\Gamma_t) = \frac{1}{1-a}\frac{W_t}{P_t}(y_t(i) + \Phi)^{\frac{a}{1-a}}. \tag{28}$$

where Γ_t indicates aggregate variables that enter into the determination of firms' marginal costs. The elasticity of the marginal cost to firm's own output is then

$$s_y(y_t(i);\Gamma_t) = \frac{a}{1-a}\left[\frac{y_t(i)}{y_t(i) + \Phi}\right]$$

which, evaluated at a steady state with symmetric prices, is

$$\overline{s}_y = \frac{a}{1-a}\left[\frac{xY}{xY + \Phi}\right] = \frac{a}{1-a}\left[\frac{x}{x + \Phi/Y}\right]. \tag{29}$$

where again $x = \psi^{-1}(1/N)$ and I denoted the steady state of aggregate output by Y. Since both x and Y are functions of N, so is $\overline{s}_y$: whether it increases or decreases with N depends upon whether x or $1/Y$ decreases more sharply with N. I discuss this point with some detail in the appendix.

We have thus established that the steady state elasticity of demand $\overline{\theta}$ is increasing in N, while the elasticity of the desired mark-up evaluated in steady state $\overline{\epsilon}_{\mu}$ is decreasing in *N*; how the elasticity of the marginal cost to firm's own output $\overline{s}_y$ depends on N is established numerically in the quantitative exercise. The overall role of N in the price/marginal cost relationship is examined next.

5.3. The Price Setting Problem

The firms pricing problem in this set up generalizes the one considered in section 4. Price setting firms at t choose their price p_t (*i*) to maximize the following expected string of profits over the life of the set price

$$E_t\left\{\sum_{j=0}^{\infty}\alpha^j Q_{t,t+j}\left[p_t(i)Y_{t+j}\,\psi'^{-1}\left(\frac{p_t(i)}{\tilde{P}_{t+j}}\right)-\mathrm{C}\left(Y_{t+j}\,\psi'^{-1}\left(\frac{p_t(i)}{\tilde{P}_{t+j}}\right);\Gamma_{t+j}\right)\right]\right\}$$

where C (.) is the firm's cost function; generalizing (4), the FOC for this problem are

$$E_t\sum_{j=0}^{\infty}\left(\begin{array}{c}\alpha^j Q_{t,t+j}P_{t+j}Y_{t+j}\,x\left(\frac{p_t(i)}{P_{t+j}}\right)\left[\theta\left(x\left(\frac{p_t(i)}{P_{t+j}}\right)\right)-1\right]\times\\ \left[\frac{p_t(i)}{P_{t+j}}-\mu\left(x\left(\frac{p_t(i)}{P_{t+j}}\right)\right)s\left(Y_{t+j}\,\psi'^{-1}\left(\frac{p_t(i)}{P_{t+j}}\right);\Gamma_{t+j}\right)\right]\end{array}\right)=0$$

where the relative share is $x\left(\frac{p}{P}\right)\equiv\psi'^{-1}\left(\frac{p}{P}\right)$. The functions θ (*x*) and $\mu(x)$ are the functions defined in (13) and (14), and *s* (yt (*i*); Γ_t) is the real marginal cost of producing quantity y_t (*i*) in period *t*, given aggregate state Γ_t, which is unaffected by the pricing decision of firm *i*.[17]

Log-linearizing the FOC around a steady state with zero inflation one obtains:

$$E_t\sum_{j=0}^{\infty}(\alpha\beta)^j\left[\begin{array}{c}\left(\widehat{p}_t^*-\Sigma_{k=1}^{j}\pi_{t+k}\right)+\overline{\epsilon}_{\mu}\overline{\theta}\left(\widehat{p}_t^*-\Sigma_{k=1}^{j}\widetilde{\pi}_{t+k}+\log\left(\frac{P_t}{\tilde{P}_t}\right)-K\right)+\\ \overline{s}_y\overline{\theta}\left(\widehat{p}_t^*-\Sigma_{k=1}^{j}\widetilde{\pi}_{t+k}+\log\left(\frac{P_t}{\tilde{P}_t}\right)-K\right)-\widehat{s}_{t+j}\end{array}\right]=0 \quad (30)$$

where $\widehat{p}_t^*=\log\left(\frac{p_t^*}{P_t}\right)-\log\left(\frac{p}{P}\right)|_{ss}$; $\pi_t\equiv\Delta\log P_t$, $\widetilde{\pi}_t\equiv\Delta\log\widetilde{P}_t$;

$K \equiv \log\left(\frac{P}{\widetilde{P}}\right)|_{ss}$; $\overline{s}_y = \frac{\partial \log s_t(i)}{\partial \log y_t(i)}|_{ss}$, $\widehat{s}_t = \log s\left(Y_t; \Gamma_t\right) - \log s\left(Y; \Gamma\right)|_{ss}$, and the study state values follow from previous calculations. In particular, from (22)

$$\log\left(\frac{p^*}{P}\right)|_{ss} = -\log\left[N\psi^{-1}\left(\frac{1}{N}\right)\right];$$

From (22) and (21)

$$\log\left(\frac{P}{\widetilde{P}}\right)|_{ss} = \log\left[N\psi^{-1}\left(\frac{1}{N}\right)\psi'\left(\psi^{-1}\left(\frac{1}{N}\right)\right)\right]$$

and since $\log s_t = \equiv \log\left(\frac{MC}{p}\frac{p}{P}\right)$ it follows that:

$$\log s\left(Y; \Gamma\right)|_{ss} = -\log \overline{\mu} - \log\left[N\psi^{-1}\left(\frac{1}{N}\right)\right]. \tag{31}$$

Log-linearizing the dynamics of the price indices, one gets, for $\widetilde{P}_t$

$$\int_0^N \left(\log p_t(i) - \log \widetilde{P}_t - \log\left[\psi'\left(\psi^{-1}\left(\frac{1}{N}\right)\right)\right]\right) di = 0$$

which to a first order approximation, gives

$$\log \widetilde{P}_t = \frac{1}{N}\int_0^N \log p_t(i)\, di - \log\left[\psi'\left(\psi^{-1}\left(\frac{1}{N}\right)\right)\right].$$

For P_t, as defined in (19), we have

$$\int_0^N \left\{\log p_t(i) - \log P_t + \log\left[N\psi^{-1}\left(\frac{1}{N}\right)\right] + \frac{\psi'(x)}{x\psi''(x)}\left(\log p_t(i) - \log \widetilde{P}_t - \log\left(\frac{p(i)}{\widetilde{P}}\right)|_{ss}\right)\right\} di = 0$$

which, to a first order approximation, implies

$$\log P_t = \frac{1}{N}\int_0^N \log p_t(i)\,di + \log\left[N\psi^{-1}\left(\frac{1}{N}\right)\right]. \tag{32}$$

Therefore, to a first order approximation,

$$\log\left(P_t/\widetilde{P}_t\right) = \log\left[N\psi^{-1}\left(\frac{1}{N}\right)\right] + \log\left[\psi'\left(\psi^{-1}\left(\frac{1}{N}\right)\right)\right] \equiv K$$

and therefore

$$\widetilde{\pi}_t = \pi_t.$$

Under the assumption of Calvo staggered prices, we can also write the expression for the general price level (32) as

$$\begin{aligned}
\log P_t &= \frac{1}{N}\left(\alpha\int_0^N \log p_{t-1}(i)\,di\right) + (1-\alpha)\log p_t^* + \log\left[N\psi^{-1}\left(\frac{1}{N}\right)\right] \\
&= \alpha\log P_{t-1} + (1-\alpha)\left(\log p_t^* + \log\left[N\psi^{-1}\left(\frac{1}{N}\right)\right]\right) \\
&= \alpha\log P_{t-1} + (1-\alpha)\left(\widehat{p}_t^* + \log P_t\right)
\end{aligned}$$

where the last equality follows from the definition of $\widehat{p}_t^*$. We then have

$$\alpha\log P_t = \alpha\log P_{t-1} + (1-\alpha)\widehat{p}_t^*. \tag{33}$$

5.4. The Slope of the NKPC

The log-linearized equilibrium conditions (30) and (33) can now be expressed, respectively, as

$$E_t \sum_{j=0}^{\infty} (\alpha\beta)^j \left[\left(1 + \overline{\theta}\left(\overline{\epsilon}_\mu + \overline{s}_y\right) \left(\widehat{p}_t^* - \sum\nolimits_{k=1}^{j} \pi_{t+k}\right) - \widehat{s}_{t+j}\right)\right] = 0 \tag{34}$$

and

$$\pi_t = \frac{1-\alpha}{\alpha} \widehat{p}_t^*. \tag{35}$$

With typical transformations, (34) and (35) imply again an expression for inflation of the form

$$\pi_t = \zeta \widehat{s}_t + \beta E_t \pi_{t+1}$$

where, however, the slope is now defined as in (11), and more explicitly as

$$\zeta = \frac{(1-\alpha\beta)(1-\alpha)}{\alpha} \frac{1}{1 + \overline{\theta}(N)\left[\overline{\epsilon}_\mu(N) + \overline{s}_y(N)\right]}. \tag{36}$$

Through the terms $\overline{\epsilon}_\mu$, $\overline{s}_y$ and $\overline{\theta}$ the slope ζ depends upon the number of goods traded in steady state.[18] As we discussed, $\overline{\theta}$ is increasing in N while $\overline{\epsilon}_\mu$ is decreasing in N, and the elasticity $\overline{s}_y$ will be shown to be as well decreasing in N. The net effect of a change in the steady state value of traded goods on the slope depends on the relative size of the changes in all these variables. This is what I analyze next.

6. Quantitative Effect of Trade Increase on the PC Slope

In order to evaluate the quantitative impact of the trade increase on the slope ζ, I need to parametrize the function $\psi^{-1}(x)$. First, I choose a functional form along the lines of Dotsey and King (2005), setting:

$$\psi(x) = \frac{1}{(1+\eta)\gamma}\left[(1+\eta)x - \eta\right]^{\gamma} - \frac{1}{(1+\eta)\gamma}(-\eta)^{\gamma},$$

where the constant term is chosen to satisfy the condition $\psi'(0) = 0$ stated above. For this form of $\psi'(x)$ the demand function (16) is derived as

$$\frac{c_t(i)}{C_t} = \frac{1}{1+\eta}\left[\left(\frac{p_t(i)}{\tilde{P}_t}\right)^{\frac{1}{\gamma-1}} + \eta\right].$$

which is a sum of a constant and a Dixit-Stiglitz term, and where the parameters γ and η control the elasticity and the curvature of the function. I discuss later the choice of particular values for the parameters γ and η that I use for the quantitative exercise.

Using the derivations of the previous section, I can now write explicit expressions for the variables that enter the slope of the Phillips curve that show how they depend on N in a steady state with symmetric prices. The steady state relative share x in (20) is

$$x \equiv \psi'^{-1}\left(\frac{1}{N}\right) = \frac{1}{1+\eta}\left\{\left(\frac{(1+\eta)\gamma}{N} + (-\eta)^{\gamma}\right)^{\frac{1}{\gamma}} + \eta\right\}; \tag{37}$$

the steady state elasticity (23) is

$$\bar{\theta} = \frac{\eta - (1+\eta)\psi'^{-1}(1/N)}{(\gamma-1)(1+\eta)\,\psi'^{-1}(1/N)}. \tag{38}$$

and the elasticity of mark-up (25) is the following function of N:

$$\bar{\epsilon}_{\mu} = \frac{\eta(\gamma-1)(1+\eta)\,\psi'^{-1}(1/N)}{\left(\eta - (1+\eta)\psi'^{-1}(1/N)\right)\left(\eta - \gamma(1+\eta)\psi'^{-1}(1/N)\right)}.$$

Finally, the steady state mark-up is

$$\bar{\mu} = \frac{\eta - (1+\eta)\psi^{-1}(1/N)}{\eta - \gamma(1+\eta)\psi^{-1}(1/N)}.$$

By calibrating values for the parameters η and γ, we can evaluate the quantitative effect of an increase in N on the slope of the inflation - marginal cost function.

Unfortunately the literature doesn't offer much guidance for what are the most plausible values for η and γ. One possibility is to choose a combination of these two parameters that guarantees a desired value for the mark-up (hence for the demand elasticity) in a steady state where the relative share x is equal to 1. Dotsey and King (2005), for example, set $\gamma = 1.02$, and determine η so that $\bar{\theta}$ (1) = 10 (or a mark up of 11%), which gives $\eta = -6$.[19] Levin et al. (2006), in order to have a markup of 16% in their baseline case, choose instead a lower value for the demand elasticity at 1, setting $\bar{\theta}$ (1) = 7, and set $\eta = -2$. In an open economy model Gust et al. (2006) choose η to match their model's implications for the volatility of output, and then select γ to give a 20% markup pricing in steady state (and $\bar{\theta}$ (1) = 6). This implies setting $\gamma = 1.15$ and $\eta = -1.87$. The larger is η in absolute value, the more concave is the demand function. This is shown in figure 1 for the case in which $\bar{\theta}$ (1) = 7, and in figure 2 for the case of $\bar{\theta}$ (1) = 10. The red line with circles in each figure corresponds to $\eta = 0$, which is the Dixit-Stiglitz constant elasticity case.

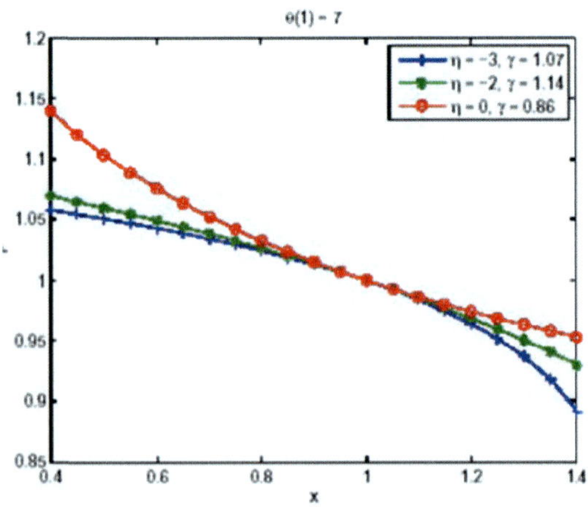

Figure 1. Demand functions for various parametrizations; $\bar{\theta}$ $(x) = 7$ at $x = 1$.

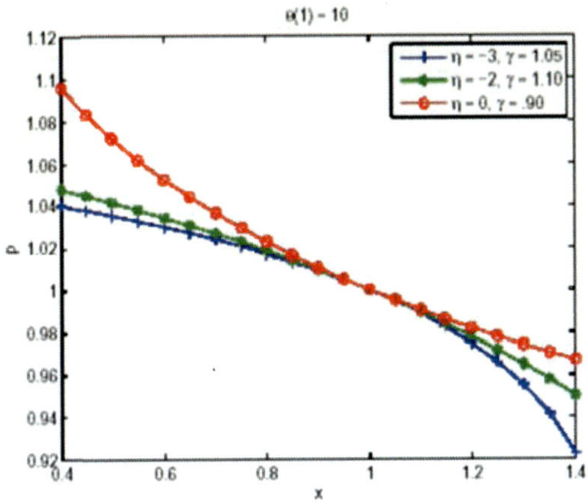

Figure 2. Demand functions for various parametrizations; $\bar{\theta}$ (x) = 10 at x = 1.

I will start by considering the implications of the parametrization of Levin et al. (2006), and then evaluate the case of a lower initial mark-up, as assumed in the parametrization of Dotsey and King. Both these parametrizations assume an elasticity at the point of unit market share relatively in line with constant elasticity estimates obtained from macro data.[20]

With micro data, however, the estimate of the elasticity of substitution depends on the level of aggregation. Broda and Weinstein (2006), for example, estimate elasticities for a larger number of goods at three different levels of aggregation, and found higher elasticities for more disaggregated sectors, showing that varieties are more close substitute when disaggregation is higher. Although their estimated elasticities cover a wide range of values, the median elasticities for the period 1972-88 range from 2.5 to 3.7, depending on the aggregation level.[21] This suggests to investigate as well the effects of parametrizations based on the assumption of a much lower elasticity in the initial steady state: by identifying this state with the period 1972-1988, which represents a pre-globalization period, I consider the case of $\bar{\theta}$ (1) = 3. Figure 3 shows the demand functions for this case, in a manner analogous to Þgures 1 and 2.

As for the choice of the two parameters η and γ, for each of the assumed initial values of $\bar{\theta}$, I choose two alternative values for η, −3 and −2, as reported in the Þgures: more negative values would make the demand curve too kinked. Given η, a value for γ follows from expression (23) evaluated at $x = 1$.

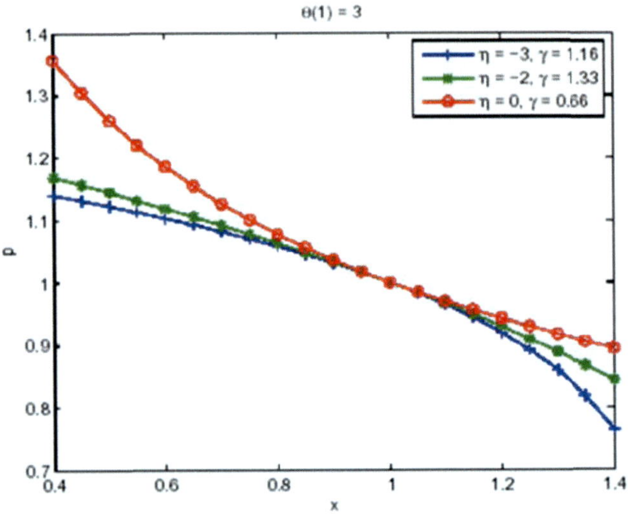

Figure 3. Demand functions for various parametrizations; $\bar{\theta}$ $(x) = 3$ at $x = 1$.

Figure 4 shows the various components of the 'strategic complementarity' term of the slope and the slope itself, for a given nominal rigidity component,[22] adopting the parametrization of Levin et al. (2006).[23] The graph on the top-left corner shows the market share as function of traded goods, $x = \psi^{-1}$ (1/N)); the following graphs show the steady state demand elasticity $\bar{\theta}$, the mark up $\bar{\mu}$, the markup elasticity $\bar{\epsilon}_\mu$, the elasticity of the marginal cost to output $\bar{s}_y$, and the Phillips curve slope ζ, all as functions of the number of traded goods N, which is on the horizontal axis (the functions are all evaluated at $x = \psi^{-1}$ $(1/N)$). The curves with crosses depict the case of a more concave demand ($\eta = -3$, and $\gamma = 1.07$); the starred curves correspond to a less concave demand function ($\eta = -2$, and $\gamma = 1.14$). Note how the decline in the desired mark-up is consistent with the evidence that an increase in trade is making the economy more competitive, as documented for example by Chen, Imbs and Scott (2006) for European countries.

The behavior of the real rigidity component of the slope depends on how the two products $\bar{\theta}\bar{\epsilon}_\mu$ and $\bar{s}_y\bar{\theta}$, which are on the denominator of expression (36), vary with the number of traded goods N. For both the chosen parametrizations in the figure, the demand elasticity $\bar{\theta}$ (graph on the top right corner) increases almost linearly in N, and the elasticity $\bar{s}_y$ (graph on the bottom left of the figure) decreases almost linearly in *N*. The mark-up elasticity $\bar{\epsilon}_\mu$ is a convex function of *N*, which declines quite rapidly as N increases from low values in the case of a more concave demand function (the blue curves with crosses). This sharp decline in $\bar{\epsilon}_\mu$ causes a decline in the product $\bar{\theta}\bar{\epsilon}_\mu$ which, at low values of N, dominates the increase in the term $\bar{s}_y\bar{\theta}$ determining a moderate increase in the slope for these values. In the case of a less concave function, as the green lines with stars show, the two terms $\bar{\theta}\bar{\epsilon}_\mu$ and $\bar{s}_y\bar{\theta}$ offset one another, so that at low values of *N* the slope curve is essentially unchanged, and then it declines monotonically. For large enough values of *N*, however, the slope declines regardless of the concavity of the demand function.

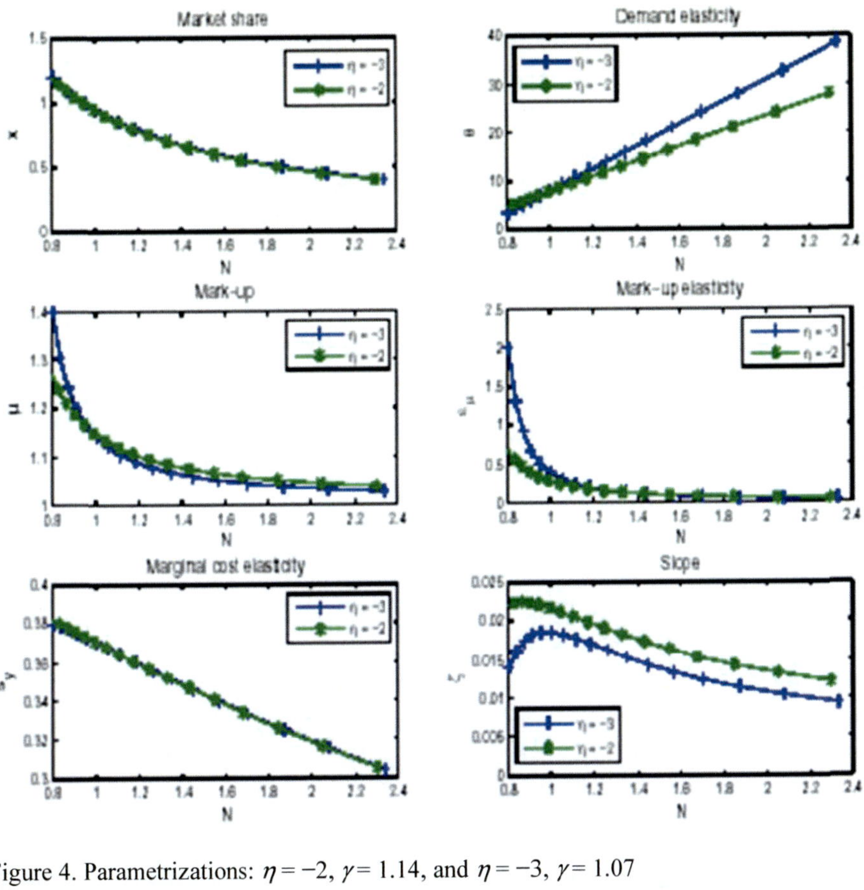

Figure 4. Parametrizations: $\eta = -2$, $\gamma = 1.14$, and $\eta = -3$, $\gamma = 1.07$

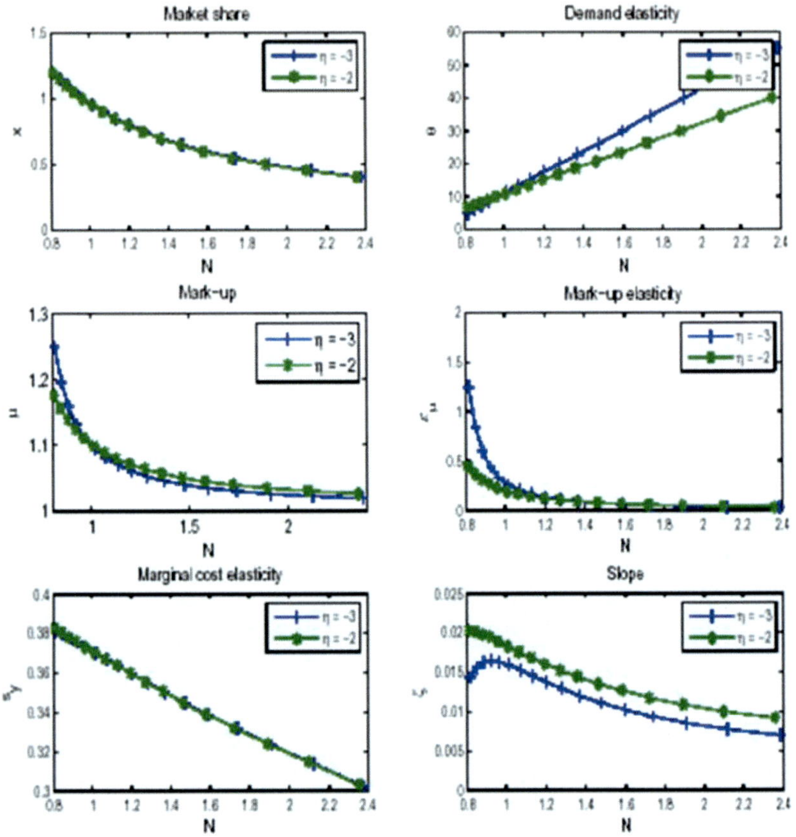

Figure 5. Parametrizations: $\eta = -2$, $\gamma = 1.10$, and $\eta = -3$, $\gamma = 1.05$.

To evaluate how sensitive this outcome is to different specifications of the parameters of the aggregator function, the next two figures plot the behavior of the same variables for the two alternative parametrizations discussed: one obtained by imposing that the parameters deliver a lower mark-up in the steady state with unit market share (the Dotsey-King case), the other where the initial steady state mark-up is very high (the case of Broda-Weinstein). The specific calibrations of the parameters η and γ are indicated in each figure.

Figure 5 plots the same variables as in figure 4 for a combination of parameters η and γ that deliver a demand elasticity $\overline{\theta} = 10$ at $x = 1$. As the figure shows, this case is relatively similar to the previous one, except that the term $\overline{\theta}\varepsilon_\mu$ has a weaker effects of the slope, reducing the extent to which the slope increases when N increases near the low initial level.

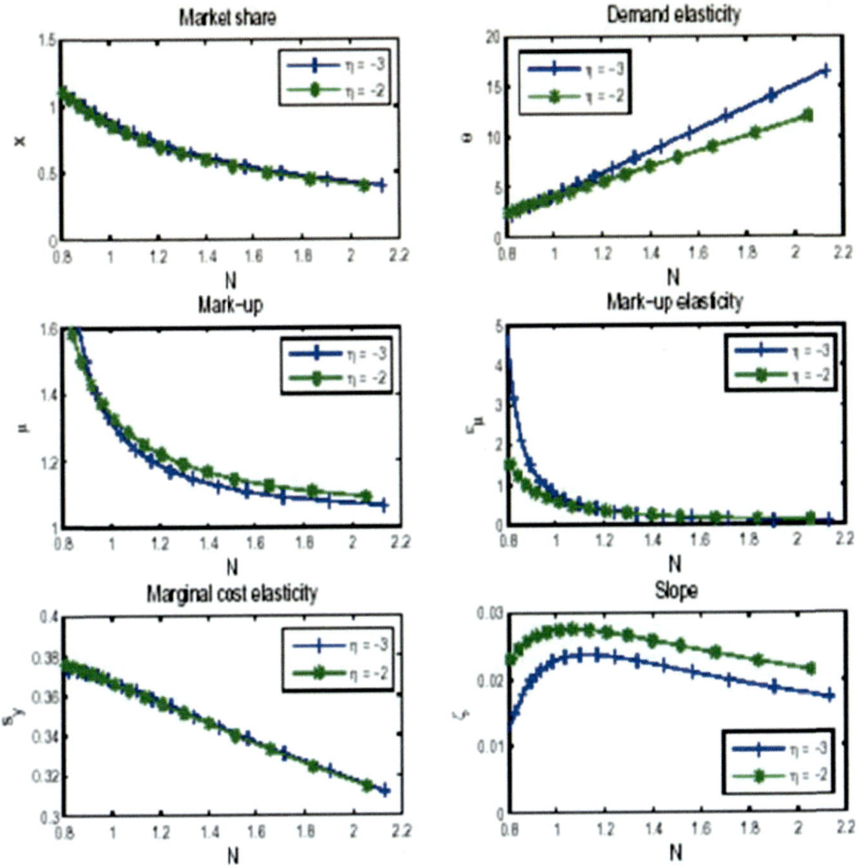

Figure 6. Parametrizations: $\eta = -2$, $\gamma = 1.33$, and $\eta = -3$, $\gamma = 1.16$.

Larger differences can instead be observed for the case where the aggregator function is parametrized to deliver a smaller elasticity in the steady state with unit market share ($\overline{\theta}$ (1) = 3) . This case is reported in figure 6.

The figure shows that the elasticity of demand increases at a slower rate with the increase in *N*, and the mark-up elasticity, which is very high at the initial steady state, declines very sharply when *N* increases: this decline makes the term $\overline{\theta}\epsilon_{\mu}$ dominate once again the behavior of the slope. As the graph on the bottom right shows, in this case the slope increases for a larger range of values of *N* for both parametrizations, and more markedly so the more concave is the demand function. Also, as *N* grows the slope eventually declines but, for the range of values considered in the Þgure, it remains always above its initial value.

6.1. Measuring the Trade Increase

The previous figures illustrate how moving from a steady state with low N to a steady state with high N has a potential effect on the slope of the NK Phillips curve. However, the assessment of the magnitude of the change in the slope is sensitive to the parametrization of the demand curve. And, within each parametrization, it matters how big is the level of traded goods that characterizes the new steady state, because of the non monotonicity of the slope function ζ. Hence, in order to make a quantitative assessment of the impact of the increase in market competition on the new Keynesian Phillips curve trade-off, one has to measure the size of the increase in trade associated with the globalization of the '90 in a way appropriate to represent the variable N of the model.

US goods imports have significantly increased in the 1960-2006 period. Figure 7 shows that the share of goods imports on GDP went from a little more than 4 percent in 1960 to about 22 percent by the end of 2006, with an increase from about 12 to 22 percent since 1989. For this latest period, however, the increase in import share excluding oil products is more modest going from about 8 to 12 percent.

The model however associates the increase in competition with an increase in the number of goods traded in the economy. For this purpose a more appropriate measure is provided by the number of varieties, as reported in the study by Broda and Weinstein (2006), which addresses the issue of the effect of globalization on trade.

Broda and Weinstein study the period 1972-2001, which they divide in two sub-periods, 1972-1988 and 1990-2001, and for each of them they report the number of varieties traded.[24] From 1990 to 2001 they register an increase in the total varieties of goods available to consumers of about 42% : the number of varieties went from approximately 182,000 to about 259,000 (table I of the paper). They observe, though, that a large number of varieties have a very small market share: to correct for a possible bias, they also provide a measure of value-weighted varieties. Under this measure, the increase in varieties is much smaller, of the order of 5 percent.[25] In the quantitative exercise I conduct below I take these two numbers as rough measures of the increase in the number of goods N to evaluate the effect of such increases on the degree of competitiveness and on the slope of the Phillips curve.

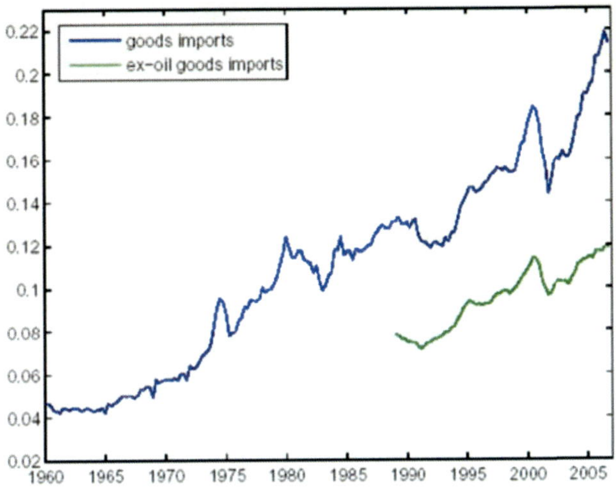

Figure 7. Goods Imports / GDP ratios, 1960 – 2006

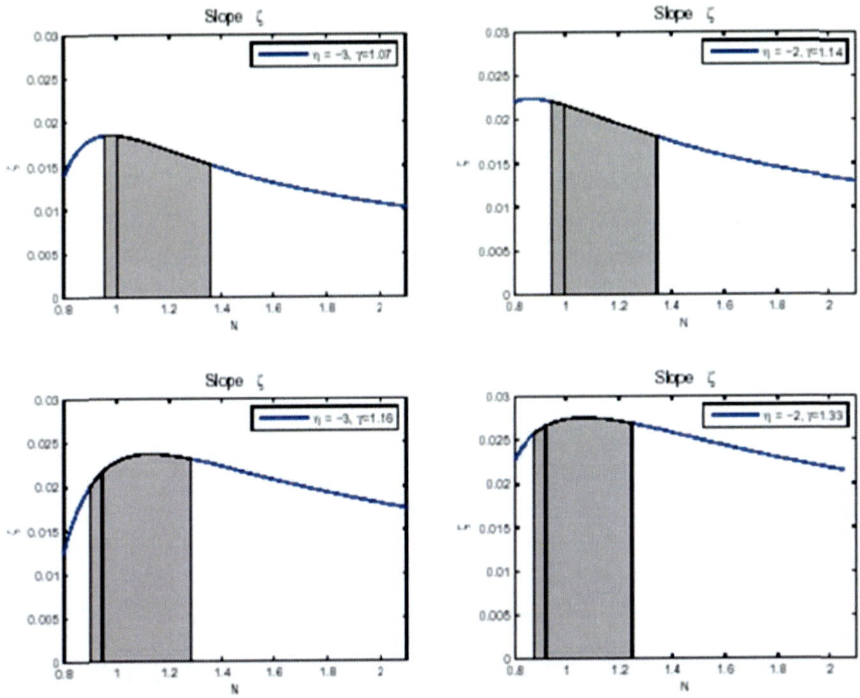

Figure 8. Effect of N on the slope ζ

The first row of figure 8 reproduces the slope obtained under the two parametrizations of the aggregator function reported in figure 4. Consider first the case of $\eta = -3$ (the graph on the left): if we characterize the initial steady state as one where the relative share is x = 1, then in this steady state the number of goods traded is approximately $N = 1/\psi'(x) = .96$, while by construction the elasticity of demand at that point is $\bar{\theta} = 7$. As discussed, the increase in the quantity of traded goods documented by Broda and Weinstein (2006) is of the order of 5 percent in terms of the value-weighted measure, but of about 42 percent without the weight. The shaded area between the first two vertical lines (from left to right) indicates the effect of moving from the initial steady state to a new steady state with a number of traded goods 5 percent higher. The vertical line farther to the right indicates a new steady state where the number of traded goods is instead 42 higher than the initial value. As the graph shows, a 5 percent increase in N is too small a change to affect the size of the slope: the decline in the product $\overline{\theta}\overline{\epsilon}_{\mu}$ is almost entirely offset by the increase in the term $\overline{s}_y\overline{\theta}$, so that the slope is essentially unchanged for these low values of N (ζ = .0185). A 42 percent increase, on the other hand, generates an overall increase in the term $(\overline{\epsilon}_{\mu} + \overline{s}_y)\overline{\theta}$ (the decline in the component $\overline{\theta}\overline{\epsilon}_{\mu}$ is more than offset by the increase in $\overline{s}_y\overline{\theta}$) so that the slope declines from about 0.0185 to 0.015. In the case of a less concave demand function (graph on the upper right) even a small increase in the steady state value of N has the effect of lowering the value of the slope. In this case, in fact, the increase in the component $\overline{s}_y\overline{\theta}$ dominates the 'real rigidity' component of the slope, making ζ smaller for any value of N larger than the initial value (the maximum decline of the slope is from 0.022 to 0.0181).

The quantitative assessment that emerges from the second row of figure 8 is quite different. Here I report how the PC slope varies with N in the two parametrizations considered in figure 6, which, relative to the previous case, start from a lower steady state elasticity (θ (1) = 3). As in the row above, the slope in the left graph is obtained from a parametrization which corresponds to a more concave demand function, relative to the one on the right. In both cases, as we observed from the discussion in the previous section, the slope tends to raise with N for a large range of values. In the initial steady state the slope is about 0.019; in a steady state where N is only 5 percent higher, the slope raises to 0.021, and in a steady state where N is almost twice as high the slope would be 0.023. The result is very similar in the case of a less concave demand function (graph on the bottom right of the figure), although the size of the slope in this case is higher for all values of N.

Overall, according to the model presented, it would be difficult to argue that the increase in trade observed in the '90s in the US should have generated an increase in competition that could lead to a decline in the slope of the inflation/ marginal cost relation. It is indeed quite possible that the increased competition has instead resulted in an increase in the slope. Moreover, this conclusion is obtained without allowing for any increase in the frequency of price adjustment in a more competitive environment, of the kind hypothesized by Rogoff (2003). Note, however, that since one is comparing two different steady states, the results depend very critically on the curvature of the demand function in the initial steady state, and on how far the new steady state is from the initial one.

7. Conclusion

In this paper I discuss whether globalization, by generating an increase in market competition, has the potential of reducing the inflation output trade-off, namely whether it is responsible for the flattening the Phillips curve that many empirical analyses suggest occurred in the past twenty years or so.

I use the Calvo model of inflation dynamics to disentangle the components of this tradeoff, and focus on the relationship between inflation and marginal costs. To analyze how this relationship, which I call the relevant 'slope', is affected by trade and market competition I depart from the model's traditional assumption of a constant elasticity of demand, making this elasticity depend instead on the relative market share of the differentiated goods. When trade moves the economy from a steady state with low trade to one with higher trade, the elasticity of demand facing the firms increases, but the elasticity of the desired mark-up declines. The balance of these two forces is the key element determining how the degree of strategic complementarity, and with it the inflation-marginal costs component of the Phillips curve slope, vary.

I argue that it is not clear that the trade increase observed in the globalization period is strong enough to have generated a decline in this component of the slope. When marginal cost is related to output, there is a further effect of the trade increase on the overall slope, since in the model the elasticity of marginal cost to aggregate output comprises the elasticity $\bar{s}_y$ which is indeed a decreasing function of number of traded goods. This effect is, however, quantitatively small, as the figures show.

A proper analysis of all the effects of a more integrated economy on the inflation-output trade-off would require to move more clearly to an open-economy setup, which would allow one to account for the price dynamics of goods produced abroad and consumed, as final or intermediate goods, in the domestic economy. As it has been shown (see for example Razin and Yuen 2002) the open economy Phillips curve is flatter than the curve of a closed economy, even in the presence of a constant elasticity of marginal cost to output, because the overall slope is declining in a trade openness parameter. My analysis could be interpreted as an analysis of the effects of increase in competition, for a given degree of openness of the economy, when an increase in the actual trade takes place.

That said, it doesn't necessarily mean that globalization had no effect on inflation dynamics. Throughout my analysis I maintain the nominal rigidity component of the slope unchanged. This is not because the frequency of price changes is unaffected by a more global environment. It is simply because it is reasonable to assume that it is not the amount of trade per se that should induce a more frequent adjustment of prices. Price stickiness is instead typically motivated by re-optimization costs, which are essentially driven by the cost of gathering information.

Moreover, the claims that globalization affect the frequency of price adjustment go both ways. On one hand, Rogoff (2003) argues that globalization has led to greater price flexibility - in the model this translates in a lower α, hence in a steepening of the curve. On the other hand, if globalization has brought an overall lower level of inflation, as argued by many, than there is less incentive to revise prices often, because the cost of price misalignment is lower. Endogeneizing the frequency of price adjustment is indeed an active area of research.

REFERENCES

[1] Bakhshi, H., Khan, H. & Burriel-Lombart, P. (forthcoming) The new Keynesian Phillips curve under trend-inflation and strategic complementarity, *Journal of Macroeconomics*.

[2] Ball, L. (2006). Has Globalization Changed Inflation?, *NBER* wp 12687.

[3] Benassy, J-P. (1996). Taste for variety and optimum production patterns in monopolistic competition, *Economics Letters 52*, 41-47.

[4] Bernanke, B. Globalization and Monetary Policy (2006). *Speech at the Fourth Economic Summit*, Stanford Institute for Economic Policy Research,

Stanford, March.

[5] Bilbiie, F. O., Ghironi, F. & Melitz, M. J. (2006a). *Endogenous Entry, Product Variety and Business Cycle*, unpublished.

[6] Bilbiie, F. O., Ghironi, F. & Melitz, M. J. (2006b). Monopoly Power and Endogenous Variety in Dynamic Stochastic General Equilibrium: *Distortions and Remedies*, unpublished.

[7] Borio, C. & Filardo A. (2007). Globalization and Inflation: New cross-country evidence on the global determinants of domestic inflation. *BIS*, unpublished.

[8] Broda,C. & Weinstein, D. (2006). Globalization and the Gains from Variety, *Quarterly Journal of Economics, 121(2)*

[9] Chen, N., Imbs, J. & Scott, A. (2006). *Competition, Globalization and the Decline of Inflation*, CEPR discussion paper n. 4695.

[10] Cogley, T. & Sbordone A. M. (2005). *A search for a structural Phillips curve*. Federal Reserve Bank of New York Staff Reports No. 203.

[11] Eichenbaum, M. & Fisher, J. (2007). Estimating the frequency of price re-optimization in Calvo-style models. *Journal of Monetary Economics*.

[12] Dotsey, M. & King, R. (2005). Implications of state-dependent pricing for dynamic macroeconomic models. *Journal of Monetary Economics 52* (1), 213-242.

[13] Dotsey, M., King, R. & Wolman A. (1999). State-dependent pricing and the general equilibrium dynamics of money and output. *Quarterly Journal of Economics 114* (3), 655-690.

[14] Gali, J. & Monacelli, T. (2005). Monetary Policy and Exchange Rate Volatility in a Small Open Economy. *Review of Economic Studies*, *72*, 707-734.

[15] Gust, C., Leduc S. & Vigfusson, R. J. (2006). *Trade Integration, Competition and the Decline in Exchange-Rate Pass-Through*, unpublished.

[16] Ihrig, J., Kamin, S. B., Lindner, D. & Marquez, J. *Some Simple Tests of the Globalization and Inflation Hypothesis*. Board of Governors International Finance Discussion Paper n. 893, forthcoming.

[17] International Monetary Fund. (2006). "How Has Globalization Affected Inflation?" *World Economic Outlook*, Chapter III, April.

[18] Ireland, P. (2005). *Changes in the Federal Reserve's Inflation Target: Causes and Consequences*, unpublished.

[19] Levin, A., Lopez-Salido, D. & Yun, T. (2006). *Strategic Complementarities and Optimal Monetary Policy*, unpublished.

[20] Kimball, M. S. (1995). The Quantitative Analytics of the Basic Neomonetarist Model. *Journal of Money, Credit and Banking*, *vol 27* (4),

1241-1277.

[21] Kohn, D.L. (2006). *The Effects of Globalization on Inflation and Their Implications for Monetary Policy*, Remarks at the Federal Reserve Bank of Boston's 51st Economic Conference, Chatam, Mass., June 16.

[22] Melitz, M. & Ottaviano, G. (2005). *Market Size, Trade and Productivity*, unpublished.

[23] Mishkin, R. (2007). Inflation Dynamics, *NBER working paper* n. 13147.

[24] Razin, A. & Yuen, C. (2002). The "New Keynesian" Phillips Curve: Closed Economy vs. Open Economy. *Economic Letters*, *75*, 1-9.

[25] Rogoff, K. (2003). *Globalization and Global Disinflation, Jackson Hole Symposium*, August 28-30.

[26] Rogoff, K. (2006). *Impact of Globalization on Monetary Policy, Jackson Hole Symposium*, August 24-26.

[27] Sbordone, A. M. (2002). Prices and unit labor costs: a new test of price stickiness, *Journal of Monetary Economics 49* (2).

[28] Woodford, M. (2003). *Interest and Prices. Foundations of a Theory of Monetary Policy*. Princeton University Press.

[29] Yellen, J. (2006). Monetary Policy in a Global Environment. Speech at the Conference '*The Euro and the Dollar in a Globalized Economy*' University of California at Santa Cruz, May.

8. APPENDIX

This appendix explains how I compute the elasticity of marginal cost defined in expression (29) as a function of the traded goods N. This involves computing how aggregate output Y varies with N, and calibrating the parameter Φ. From expression (28), one derives the steady state real marginal cost as

$$s = \frac{1}{1-a} w \left(xY + \Phi\right)^{\frac{a}{1-a}}, \tag{39}$$

where ω denotes the steady state real wage. Assuming a fairly standard preference specification: $u\ (C,\ h) = \log C - 1\ \frac{1}{1+\nu} h^{1+\nu}$, the real wage is $w_t = H_t^{\nu} C_t$. Aggregate hours H_t are

$$H_t = \int_0^N h_t(i)\, di = \int_0^N \left(y_t(i) + \Phi\right)^{\frac{1}{1-a}} di,$$

where I used the definition of hours in (27). Steady state aggregate hours are then

$$H = N\left(xY + \Phi\right)^{\frac{1}{1-a}},$$

which, substituted in the expression for the equilibrium real wage, allows to rewrite (39) as

$$s = \frac{1}{1-a} N^{\nu} \left(xY + \Phi\right)^{\frac{\nu+a}{1-a}} Y. \tag{40}$$

From (31) in the text the steady state real marginal cost is $s = 1/N\overline{\mu}x$. Combining this expression with (40) we obtain that

This expression defines a concave, increasing function $Y = Y(N)$. For a given calibration of the parameters a, ν and , any value of N determines a value of Y, which, together with the value of x, allows to compute a value for the elasticity $\overline{s}_y$. I set the parameter ν to be equal to 2, which corresponds to assuming a Frisch elasticity of labor supply of .5, the high end of the range typically found in micro studies; $1 - a = .68$, to roughly match the average observed labor share for the

U.S. To calibrate Φ I first use the entry condition to establish a zero-profit upper bound to the fixed cost of production:

$$\Phi^u = \frac{1}{N^{1-a}}\left(1 - \frac{1-a}{\overline{\mu}}\right)$$

Then I set Φ sufficiently close but strictly lower than Φ^u to allow entry of new firms with positive profits: $\Phi = .2$. The results are not very sensitive to the range of values chosen for these parameters, since they have mostly a scale effect on $\overline{s}_y$, and hence on ζ, without affecting its curvature.

End Notes

[1] See Woodford (2003) ch. 3. The term 'real rigidity' was introduced, I believe, by Ball and Romer (1989).

[2] See literature cited later.

[3] Several aspects of the difference between open and closed economy are discussed by Woodford (2007, in this volume).

[4] The increase in competitiveness on one hand reduces the monopoly wedge that determines the inflation bias of the central bank, and on the other makes prices and wages more flexible, reducing the real effects of unanticipated monetay policy, hence the gain from inflating.

[5] Throughout the paper I will use the term slope to indicate the elasticity of inflation to marginal cost, rather than to output.

[6] If one assumes that non re-optimized prices are indexed at least partly to trend inflation, this additional dynamics is eliminated and the slope is unaffected by the steady state inflation $\overline{\Pi}$. Models with positive trend inflation can be generalized to the case of time-varying steady state inflation; in this case the model describes the dynamics of inflation deviations from a time-varying trend: $\hat{\pi}_t = \ln(\Pi_t/\overline{\Pi}_t))$. Cogley-Sbordone (2005) estimate a NKPC with time-varying trend inflation. Ireland (2006) and Smets and Wouters (2003), among others, estimate general equilibrium models in the new Keynesian literature allowing for a time varying trend inflation; their assumptions however deliver a time-invariant slope.

[7] For evidence from survey data see for example, Blinder et al. (1998).

[8] Sbordone (2002) discusses this case. A more sophisticated model assumes that capital is endogenously determined, and its limited reallocation is due to the existence of adjustment costs. Woodford (2005) discusses this model, and concludes that the hypothesis of a fixed capital is a good enough approximation. For another empirical application, see Eichenbaum and Fisher (2007).

[9] For example, with a Cobb-Douglas production technology $s\,y = a/\,(1 - a)$, where $1 - a$ is the output elasticity with respect to labor.

[10] See the discussion of these preferences in the context of models with price rigidities in Woodford (2003).

[11] See the later derivation for the specific parametrization considered

12 Note that under this assumption changes in the number of goods available for sale involve no change in preferences as the utility function is independent of N. This contrast with Benassy's (1996) generalization of the Dixit-Stiglitz preferences, that depend on the value N.

13 The function θ (.) could also be expressed as a function of the relative price, rather than the market share, as in Gust et al. (2006).

14 Note that this elasticity could alternatively defined as $\epsilon_{\mu}(x) = -\epsilon_{\theta}(x)/[\theta(x) - 1]$ where $\epsilon_{\theta}(x) = \frac{\partial \log \theta(x)}{\partial \log x}$.

15 The value of $\overline{\epsilon}_{\mu}$ is important to determine the degree of strategic complementarities in price setting, for small departures from the uniform-price steady state (see Woodford 2003).

16 This follows from the hypothesis that $\theta'(x) <0$, so that $\mu(x)$ is an increasing function of x. In this case it is not possible for log μ to be a concave function of log x, because this would require log μ to be negative for positive, and small enough x. But this can't happen, no matter how large $\theta(x)$ gets for small x. If log μ must be convex at least for small values of x, it is convenient to assume that it is a globally convex function of log$x$.

17 Note that the real marginal cost is defined as the ratio $MC_t(i)/P_t$, not the ratio $MC_t(i)/\widetilde{P}_t$.

18 It should also be observed that Nhas an additional e.ect on the inflation dynamics that can be seen by rewriting (6) as

$$\pi_t = \zeta(\log s_t - \log \overline{s}) + \beta E_t \pi_{t+1}.$$

The steady state value of the marginal cost is function of the steady state mark-up $\overline{\mu}$ and the steady state relative price p/P, both functions of N $\log \overline{s}(N) = -\log \overline{\mu}(N) - \log\left[N\psi^{-1}\left(\frac{1}{N}\right)\right]$

19 It follows from (23) that for x= 1: $\overline{\theta} = \frac{-1}{(\gamma-1)(1+\eta)}$. ▷

20 At the macro level, Cogley-Sbordone (2005) estimate a Calvo model with a Dixit-Stiglitz specification and time-varying inflation trend; they estimate the Dixit-Stiglitz elasticity using aggregate data on inflation, unit labor costs, output and interest rates across subperiods (chosen a priori as representing periods of di.erent steady state inflation). They do not find evidence that the elasticity di.ers across the subsamples, which cover pre and post 1990, and estimate an elasticity of about 10.

21 It's also interesting to note that their estimated elasticities, across each disaggregation group, rather than increase, appear to decrease, albeit slightly, in the 1990-2001 period versus the 1972-1988. Their interpretation is that imported goods have become more differentiated over time.

22 Recall that this term is defined as $\frac{(1-\alpha)(1-\alpha\beta)}{\alpha}$ and doesn't depend on N. I calibrate $\beta = .99$ and $\alpha = .7$, which corresponds to an average interval of 9-10 months between price changes.

23 That is, the combinations of the parameters η and γ are such that the demand elasticity in a steady state with unit market share is equal to 7.

24 They define a variety as "import of a particular good from a particular country" (p. 550) and use two different sources for each subperiod (data on 1989 are not included because of the unification of Germany in that year, which makes the data not comparable with those of the following years).

25 This is obtained from the reported γ ratio in table VII of Broda-Weinstein (2006). The gross increase in varieties is computed as the inverse of the (median) γ ratio reported for the corrected count and for the one in table I.

In: Financial Globalization
Editor: Jason H. Cardwell

ISBN: 978-1-60692-190-6

Chapter 2

FINANCIAL GLOBALIZATION AND THE U.S. CURRENT ACCOUNT DEFICIT*

Matthew Higgins and Thomas Klitgaard

Despite heavy borrowing in recent years, the United States has financed its large current account deficits without experiencing an unusual buildup in foreign investors' holdings of U.S. assets. A new analysis suggests that this somewhat surprising development is attributable largely to rapid financial globalization, with cross-border flows worldwide rising as fast as flows into the United States. However, it could be harder for the country to sustain large deficits on favorable terms if the current wave of globalization subsided or the rate at which U.S. investors buy foreign assets increased.

To finance its large current account deficit, the United States must attract the equivalent amount of surplus foreign savings. In recent years, the U.S. deficit has been large enough to absorb the lion's share of surpluses generated abroad. Indeed, from 1999 through 2006, the cumulative U.S. borrowing of $4.4 trillion amounted to some 85 percent of the net external financing provided by countries with surplus saving.

Despite this heavy borrowing, however, the United States has been the destination for little more than 30 percent of total gross cross-border investments

---

* This is an edited, reformatted and augmented version of a Federal Reserve Bank of New York publication dated December 2007.

by other countries, a figure that only slightly exceeds the U.S. share of global GDP and is below the U.S. weight in global financial portfolios. As a result, the United States has been able to finance its large current account deficits without laying claim to a disproportionate share of global foreign investment or causing foreign external portfolios to become dominated by U.S. assets.

This edition of *Current Issues* sheds light on these seemingly incompatible developments by examining the financing of the U.S. current account deficit from a global perspective. We find that the recent period of large U.S. current account deficits has also been one of rapid financial globalization, with surplus and deficit countries alike investing a record fraction of their saving abroad. This sharp increase in cross-border investments has made it possible for the United States to emerge as the world's principal net borrower while receiving an unremarkable share of other countries' gross external investments. Facilitating this development is the fact that the rise in U.S. cross-border investment has lagged the rise in global investment by other countries.

These findings have important implications for the sustainability of the U.S. current account deficit. In our view, it might be harder to finance continued large current account deficits on favorable terms if the recent wave of financial globalization were to subside: The United States would then have to attract a larger share of other countries' foreign investments. It might also be harder to finance the deficit on favorable terms were U.S. investors to participate more fully in financial globalization by investing a larger fraction of domestic saving abroad.

Global Saving and Global Capital Flows

A country's current account balance is equal to the difference between domestic saving and domestic investment spending. A country that saves more than it invests at home sends its surplus abroad to purchase foreign assets. One that saves less than it invests finances the shortfall by issuing liabilities to foreign investors. The accumulated history of current account surpluses or deficits, along with capital gains and losses on past investments, determines a country's net international investment position.

However, the *net* flow of capital across international borders often comes alongside much larger gross flows. After all, even countries running current account surpluses receive foreign investment inflows, and even countries running deficits invest abroad. Thus, the current account balance also obeys the accounting identity:

CA balance = domestic purchases of foreign assets
- foreign purchases of domestic assets.[1]

Analysis of the sustainability of large U.S. current account deficits generally focuses on the implied behavior of U.S. net international liabilities. There is good reason for this emphasis. Formally, sustainability requires a path for the deficit that keeps net liabilities from rising indefinitely as a share of GDP. More concretely, continued deficits of the recent scale would likely push U.S. net liabilities as a share of GDP to an unprecedented level for a large advanced economy—a prospect that naturally raises concerns about whether such a trajectory would be compatible with economic and financial stability.[2] Moreover, investors' knowledge or belief that a substantially weaker dollar may be required to hold U.S. net liabilities to a sustainable path could lead to a general attempt to reduce U.S. exposures in advance of the dollar's fall, potentially setting off sudden and disruptive dollar adjustment.

However, the behavior of *gross* foreign claims on the United States is also important for sustainability analysis. After all, the capital losses that foreign investors might suffer from potential dollar weakness depend on the scale of gross rather than net claims. So too do the incentive for and potential magnitude of portfolio repositioning given a reassessment of risk and return on dollar assets.

In this connection, concerns about U.S. current account sustainability have often been based on the premise that the U.S. deficit is causing foreign portfolios to become increasingly tilted toward dollar assets. If so, while large deficits continue, foreign investors' reluctance to see portfolios grow even more unbalanced should exert ongoing downward pressure on the dollar and other U.S. asset prices. Some see that risk-tolerance limits for dollar exposure might be close at hand. As former Federal Reserve Chairman Paul Volker (2005) colorfully put it, "At some point, both central banks and private institutions will have their fill of dollars."[3] Even many who take a more benign view of U.S. and global imbalances argue that foreign investors' desire to keep exposure to U.S. financial assets from climbing higher will act as the ultimate check on the capacity of the United States to sustain large current account deficits.[4]

In fact, foreign purchases of U.S. assets have recently been well in excess of the U.S. current account deficit (Chart 1). Since 2002, the additional foreign investment in the United States has averaged roughly 5 percent of U.S. GDP. The counterpart to this additional inflow has been a continuing flow of U.S. investment abroad. Indeed, despite considerable year-toyear volatility, outflows from the United States have generally been higher than they were before the period of large deficits. Last year saw outflows, inflows, and the current account deficit all reach record highs as shares of GDP.

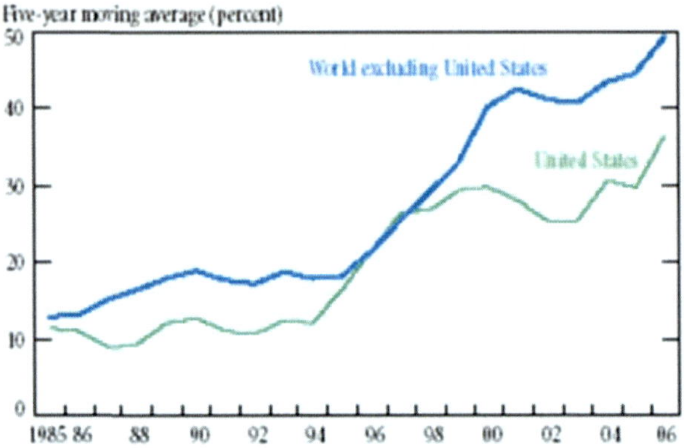

Source: U.S. Department of Commerce, Bureau of Economic Analysis.

Note: The statistical discrepancy in balance-of-payments accounts is attributed equally to outflows and inflows.

Chart 1. Financial Flows to and from the United States

The fact that foreign investment in the United States has been outpacing the U.S. current account deficit might appear to support concerns about foreign portfolios growing increasingly lopsided: Perhaps foreign investors will bump up against tolerance limits for dollar exposure that much sooner.

However, rising foreign investment in the United States does not necessarily imply a rising dollar weight in global portfolios: Flows to the United States must be rising *more rapidly* than flows to other countries (abstracting from valuation changes). To determine whether this has in fact occurred, we consider financial flows involving the United States from a global perspective. Our findings overturn the widespread presumption that global portfolios are tilting more toward claims on the United States. Rather, rising investment in the country has occurred during a period of rapid financial globalization, in the form of surging crossborder investment worldwide.

Taking the Measure of Financial Globalization

Financial globalization refers to the ongoing integration of once poorly connected national financial markets. A key aspect of globalization is a decline in financial *home bias*—the tendency for domestic saving to be invested predominantly at home, with domestic portfolios tilted heavily toward home-country assets.

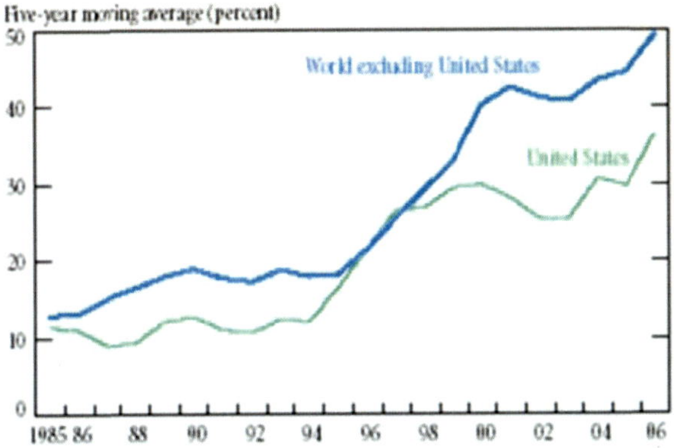

Source: International Monetary Fund, International Financial Statistics and World Economic Outlook.

Chart 2. Cross-Border Investment Share of Global Saving

Recent years have in fact seen a pronounced decline in home bias, with a record fraction of global saving going to cross-border investments (Chart 2).[5] Indeed, in 2005 and 2006, the share of global saving invested abroad climbed past 50 percent for the first time. (Chart 2 shows five-year averages, to smooth out business cycle fluctuations; thus, the values shown for 2005 and 2006 are a bit below 50 percent.) The trend toward greater cross-border investment has been worldwide, with the United States, other advanced economies, and emerging economies all investing a markedly higher fraction of saving abroad.

Significantly, U.S. external investment as a share of saving has risen less dramatically than the share for other countries. Comparing the mid-1990s with the middle of the current decade, we see that U.S. outflows as a share of domestic saving have risen by roughly 20 percentage points; the increase abroad has been close to 35 percentage points. As a result, the United States now lags the rest of the world by a considerable margin in the share of national saving invested abroad.

It is instructive to consider the smaller scale of outflows from the United States in light of the current account balanceof- payments accounting identity described earlier. In particular, had outflows from the United States risen in line with the global trend, the country would have required that much more inward investment to finance an *unchanged* sequence of current account deficits. In turn, more robust U.S. demand for foreign assets, and the consequent need to attract additional inflows, would have placed downward pressure on the dollar, leading to at least somewhat *smaller* deficits.

This scenario illustrates a more general point: developments that lead to shifts in gross capital flows have important feedback effects on *net* flows.

U.S. ASSETS IN GLOBAL PORTFOLIOS

Has the United States been receiving a disproportionate share of global cross-border investments? To answer this question, we compare the share of capital flows going to the United States with the relative size of the U.S. economy or, where possible, the size of the relevant capital market. In particular, portfolio equity and fixed-income flows are assessed relative to the U.S. share of the global equity and fixed-income markets: This is the metric Wall Street equity and fixed-income strategists use to determine whether a recommended portfolio allocation is underweight, neutral, or overweight in a given national market.[6] Unfortunately, there is no clear measure of the size of the relevant market for foreign direct investment (FDI) or banking and miscellaneous investments. However, international portfolios based on relative economic output or GDP seem a sensible choice.[7] In an investment strategy with a neutral U.S. weight, the share of cross-border investment placed in the United States would be equal to the relevant scaling factor. For example, since the United States accounts for 28 percent of global GDP, a neutral investment allocation would have the United States receiving 28 percent of the flow of global FDI investments.[8]

Using our neutral benchmark, we find that, from 2002 to 2006, foreign investors placed a total of $6.1 trillion in new investments in the United States, or slightly more than 30 percent of total outflows from countries other than the United States (Table 1). Our calculations show that a neutral investment allocation based on country GDP and market capitalization weights would have resulted in the United States receiving $7.0 trillion in foreign capital. Thus, global cross-border investments were tilted *away from* the United States, by a factor of 0.87 (that is, 6.1/7.0). Significantly, a similar tilt ratio prevailed during 1997-2001, when the U.S. current account deficit was considerably smaller, and a *higher* tilt ratio prevailed during 1992-96, when the deficit was far smaller.[9] Indeed, over the last twenty years, foreign external investments have never displayed any discernible tilt toward U.S. assets (Chart 3). Simply put, the proliferation of cross-border investment worldwide has enabled the United States to finance its growing current account deficits while receiving a stable or even declining fraction of other countries' overall external investments.

Table 1. Foreign Investment in the United States

Trillions of U.S. dollars and ratio-to-neutral allocation			
	2002-06	**1997-2001**	**1992-96**
All investments	6.1	3.7	1.7
Ratio-to-neutral	0.87	0.85	0.99
Foreign direct investment	0.6	1.1	0.3
Ratio-to-neutral	0.64	0.93	1.10
Portfolio equity	0.4	0.5	0.0
Ratio-to-neutral	0.46	0.64	0.35
Bonds	3.2	1.1	0.8
Ratio-to-neutral	1.11	0.81	0.97
Banking and other	2.0	1.0	0.6
Ratio-to-neutral	0.82	1.01	1.11

Sources: International Monetary Fund, International Financial Statistics and World Economic Outlook database; Datastream global equity indexes; Bank for International Settlements global bond database; authors' estimates.

Note: Ratio-to-neutral refers to foreign investment in the United States relative to an investment allocation proportional to country weights in global GDP or the relevant global capital market. A figure above 1.00 indicates that foreign investors have been investing relatively heavily in the United States.

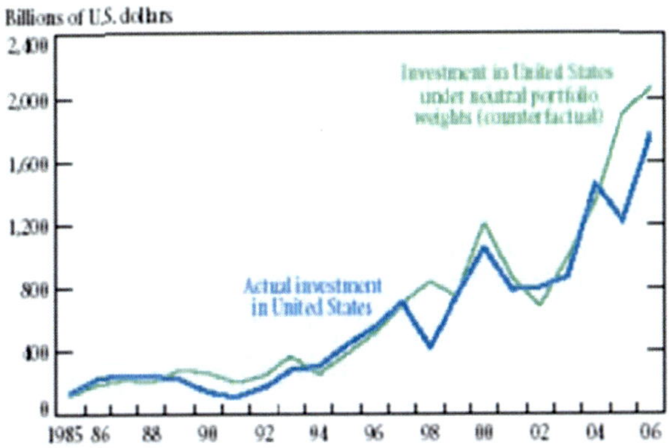

Sources: International Monetary Fund; Bank for International Settlements; U.S. Department of Commerce, Bureau of Economic Analysis; authors' calculations.

Notes: The calculation for market-neutral investment takes total outflows from other countries as given. The calculation shows the funds that would go to the United States given portfolio weights based on the U.S. weight in the global capital markets (for equity and fixed-income securities) or the U.S. weight in global GDP (for foreign direct investment and banking and other investments).

Chart 3. Foreign Investment in the United States

A broadly similar pattern is evident across asset categories. In particular, for FDI, portfolio equity investments, and banking and other investments, investment in the United States during the 2002-06 period was below our neutral benchmark, and down relative to those benchmarks from 1997 to 2001. Only fixed-income investments have recently exceeded our neutral benchmark and, even here, only slightly.

International Investment Positions

A look at international investment positions—the dollar value of external assets, rather than the flow of new external investments—supports the results of our flow analysis (Table 2).[10] In particular, other countries' external portfolios were tilted slightly toward claims on the United States in 1999, but are now tilted slightly away (1999 provides a convenient reference point, as it is the first year the data allow us to exclude from global external assets the claims of one European Economic and Monetary Union [EMU] country on another). The tilt away from the United States comes despite a near doubling of foreign ownership of U.S. assets, from $8.4 trillion to $16.2 trillion. The reason is that other countries' total cross-border asset holdings rose in even greater proportion, from $17.9 trillion to $47.5 trillion.[11]

By asset category, other countries' stocks of foreign direct investments, once sharply tilted toward the United States, now show a clear tilt away. Portfolio equity investments have shifted from being tilted slightly toward the United States to slightly away. The shift away from the country in FDI and portfolio equity holdings reflects the similar trend in flows described above as well as the relatively weak performance of the U.S. equity markets.[12]

Meanwhile, foreign investors have shifted from a somewhat underweight position in U.S. debt securities and banking and other assets to a more balanced position. The relatively modest current tilt in debt securities toward the United States reflects the explosive growth of cross-border debt security claims worldwide. While debt security claims on the United States roughly tripled over the period, so did all global cross-border holdings.

Alternative Metrics

Our analysis of foreign portfolio exposure to the United States is based on investment in the country as a fraction of global *cross-border* investments. In our view, this approach illustrates underlying trends while controlling for the ongoing progress of financial globalization. Still, a look at how exposure to the United States has evolved relative to global saving and global wealth might shed additional light on the sustainability of the U.S. current account deficit.

Since 2002, investment in the United States has absorbed 16.5 percent of the rest of the world's saving, up from 14.3 percent during 1997-2001 and up substantially from 7.0 percent during 1992-96. Is the recent figure high or low? If such investment were sustained, assuming stable exchange rates and similar asset price behavior in the United States and abroad, claims on U.S. assets would trend toward 16.5 percent of total foreign wealth. We cannot know the potential limits on desired foreign exposure to the United States; the limits depend, in part, on how far the recent wave of financial globalization can progress. That said, a 16.5 percent figure would not be out of line with the U.S. weight in the global economy and the global financial markets.

Table 2. Foreign Claims on the United States

Trillions of U.S. dollars and ratio-to-neutral allocation		
	2006	**1999**
Total claims	16.2	8.4
Ratio-to-neutral	0.94	1.08
Foreign direct investment	3.2	2.8
Ratio-to-neutral	0.77	1.56
Portfolio equity	2.5	1.5
Ratio-to-neutral	0.96	1.05
Bonds	5.7	2.1
Ratio-to-neutral	1.03	0.88
Banking and other	4.8	2.0
Ratio-to-neutral	1.00	0.86

Sources: U.S. Department of Commerce, Bureau of Economic Analysis; International Monetary Fund, International Financial Statistics and World Economic Outlook database; Datastream global equity indexes; Bank for International Settlements global bond database; authors' estimates.

Notes: Ratio-to-neutral refers to foreign claims on the United States relative to a portfolio allocation proportional to country weights in global GDP or the relevant global capital market. A figure above 1.00 indicates that other countries' external portfolios are tilted toward claims on the United States. U.S. derivative liabilities are not counted because their economic value is a small fraction of the quoted notional value.

It is important to understand what fraction of foreign wealth today is in the form of claims on the United States. Unfortunately, no comprehensive measure of foreign wealth exists.[13] The best approach we can take, then, is to consider claims on the United States relative to a measure of foreign capital market size.[14]

As an indicator of total capital market size, we take the sum of equity market capitalization, bond market capitalization, and commercial bank assets. (This approach follows the measure used in the International Monetary Fund's *Global Financial Stability Report* [2007].) We define a proxy for non-U.S. financial wealth as

Non-U.S. wealth = non-U.S. capital market size
+ claims on U.S. - liabilities to U.S.

According to our calculations, the share of non-U.S. financial wealth held as U.S. assets has *declined* very slightly in recent years, to just 12.3 percent at year-end 2006 (Table 3). We consider this small decline to be well within the margin of measurement error. In essence, growth in foreign financial market size has kept pace with growth in foreign claims on the United States. In dollar terms, non-U.S. equity market capitalization has increased by a factor of 1.6 since year-end 1999, bond market capitalization by a factor of 2.1, and commercial bank assets by a factor of 2.2. These figures also illustrate a more general point: growth in non-U.S. financial markets widens the scope for diversification into U.S. assets.

Table 3. Foreign Financial Assets and Claims on the United States

Trillions of U.S. dollars		
	2006	**1999**
Total financial assets	132.1	65.1
Percentage of claims on the United States	12.3	13.0
Equity securities	25.4	16.3
Percentage of claims on the United States	10.0	9.3
Debt securities	46.9	21.6
Percentage of claims on the United States	12.1	9.7

Sources: U.S. Department of Commerce, Bureau of Economic Analysis; International Monetary Fund, International Financial Statistics and World Economic Outlook database; Datastream global equity indexes; Bank for International Settlements global bond database; authors' estimates.

Notes: Total financial assets are the sum of portfolio equity holdings, debt security holdings, and commercial bank assets. Percentage of claims on the United States includes a correction for rest-of-the-world liabilities to the United States. The figures for equity securities represent a lower bound; see footnote 14 in the text.

Turning to tradable securities, we observe that the fraction of foreign fixed-income wealth held in claims on the United States has increased slightly in recent years, to a stilllow 12 percent at year-end 2006. Given the scale of reserve accumulation by foreign central banks, the share of foreign *private* fixed-income wealth held as claims on the United States must have declined. The fraction of portfolio equity wealth held as claims on the United States has also increased slightly in recent years, to almost 10 percent. Again, while we cannot know the amount of exposure to U.S. securities that foreign investors will eventually take on, these figures are hardly out of line with the size of the United States in the global markets.[15]

Our results should assuage concerns about large U.S. current account deficits leading to a potentially destabilizing increase in foreign exposure to U.S. assets. In fact, foreign investment in the United States has remained broadly in line with the relative size of the U.S. economy and U.S. capital markets. Moreover, foreign claims on the United States have not risen relative to cross-border claims generally or relative to the size of foreign capital markets. Of course, as we have already indicated, there may be other good reasons for concerns about the sustainability of large, ongoing U.S. current account deficits.

Financial Globalization and U.S. Current Account Adjustment

Rapid growth in cross-border investments worldwide has left room for the United States to take in large net flows while receiving an unremarkable fraction of other countries' total cross-border investments. But what if the recent wave of financial globalization were to crest? To address this question, we consider a hypothetical scenario.

In recent years, about 50 percent of non-U.S. saving has been invested abroad, and the United States has received about one-third of those outflows. Suppose that outflows were to fall back to 35 percent of saving, roughly the share of U.S. saving recently recorded for U.S. outflows. The United States would then have to receive more than 45 percent of the rest of the world's foreign investments (assuming that the U.S. current account deficit and U.S. outflows remain constant as shares of GDP and that the foreign saving rate and the relative size of U.S. and foreign economies are also constant). Under such a scenario, foreign investors would most likely require added compensation for shifting toward an overweight U.S. position in the form of higher U.S. interest rates, or more favorable entry prices via a weaker dollar or lower U.S. asset prices. (One limitation of this scenario is that it does not allow for such interest rate and asset price changes to promote a narrowing of U.S. and global imbalances.)

Fuller participation by U.S. investors in the financial globalization process could also make it more challenging to finance large current account deficits on favorable terms. Suppose that outflows from the United States were to rise to 50 percent of saving: the recent average for the rest of the world. (Given the anemic U.S. saving rate, this amount would still leave outflows from the United States unusually low as a share of GDP.) Again assuming an unchanged current account deficit, the United States would then have to receive roughly 40 percent of total outflows from the rest of the world, up from the 30 percent currently coming to the United States.

Conclusion

Perhaps surprisingly, large U.S. current account deficits have not led to an unusual buildup in foreign investors' holdings of U.S. assets; in fact, foreign investment in the United States has remained broadly in line with the relative size of the U.S. economy and the U.S. capital markets. The key reason for this outcome has been rapid financial globalization, with cross-border flows worldwide rising as fast as flows into the United States. Our results suggest that such globalization has allowed the United States to finance large current account deficits without experiencing sharper downward pressures on the dollar and U.S. asset prices. However, a retreat from the recent pace of financial globalization by foreign investors or an increase in the rate at which U.S. investors buy foreign assets could make it more difficult for the country to sustain a large current account deficit on favorable terms.

References

Athanasoulis, Stefano, Robert Shiller & Wincoop, Eric van. (1999). "Macro Markets and Financial Security." Federal Reserve Bank of New York *Economic Policy* Review 5, *no. 1* (April): 21-39.

Greenspan, Alan. (2003). "Current Account." Remarks delivered at the Twenty-First Annual Monetary Conference, cosponsored by the Cato Institute and *The Economist*, Washington, D.C., November 20.

Matthew Higgins, Klitgaard Thomas & Tille Cédric (2007). "Borrowing without Debt? Understanding the U.S. International Investment Position." *Business Economics 42*, no. 1 (January): 17-27.

Matthew Higgins & Steinberg Bruce. (2002). "Benign U.S. Current Account Deficit." *The Global Economy*, March 15. New York: Merrill Lynch & Co., Global Securities Research & Economics Group.

International Monetary Fund (2007). *Global Financial Stability Report.* Washington, D.C.

Lane, Philip, and Gian Maria Milesi-Ferretti. 2007. "A Global Perspective on External Positions." In Richard H. Clarida, ed., G7 *Current Account Imbalances: Sustainability and Adjustment*, 67-98. Chicago: University of Chicago Press.

MSCI Barra (2006). "*MSCI Global Capital Markets Index Overview.*"

Orszag, Peter R. (2007). "*Foreign Holdings of U.S. Government Securities and the U.S. Current Account.*" Testimony before the U.S. House Committee on the Budget, 110th Cong., 1st sess., June 26.

Summers, Lawrence H. (2006). *"Reflections on Global Account Imbalances and Emerging Markets Reserve Accumulation.*" L. K. Jha Memorial Lecture, delivered at the Reserve Bank of India, Mumbai, India, March 24.

Volker, Paul A. (2005). "*An Economy on Thin Ice.*" Washington Post, April 10, p. B07.

About the Authors

Matthew Higgins is an assistant vice president in the Development Studies and Foreign Research Function of the Emerging Markets and International Affairs Group; Thomas Klitgaard is an assistant vice president in the International Research Function of the Research and Statistics Group.

In: Financial Globalization
Editor: Jason H. Cardwell

ISBN: 978-1-60692-190-6

Chapter 3

FOREIGN HOLDINGS OF U.S. GOVERNMENT SECURITIES AND THE U.S. CURRENT ACCOUNT*

United States Congressional Budget Office

Chairman Spratt, Ranking Member Ryan, and Members of the Committee, thank you for inviting me to testify today. Foreign holdings of U.S. Treasury debt have grown rapidly in recent years and now are a significant percentage of such debt held by the public. A broader issue is the substantial deficit in the U.S. current account—which summarizes the country's current transactions with the rest of the world, including trade in goods and services, net income from international investments and the compensation of employees, and net unilateral transfers (such as gifts, pension payments, and foreign aid). The mirror image of the nation's large current-account deficit is foreign investors' increased holdings of a variety of claims on the United States, including U.S. government debt as well as privatesector securities and assets.

My testimony today makes four main points:

---

* This is an edited, reformatted and augmented version of a Congressional Budget Office publication dated June 2007.

Foreign holdings of U.S. Treasury debt have risen rapidly. Between 2003 and 2006, for example, such holdings rose almost 50 percent. They now exceed $2 trillion and account for more than 40 percent of Treasury debt held by the public.

Those increasing foreign holdings of U.S. government debt are part of a more fundamental issue: The nation is running a substantial current-account deficit, which is financed by increasing liabilities to and assets held by foreign investors. The current-account deficit measures the excess of the country's spending over its income or, equivalently, of its domestic investment over its national saving. After the depreciation of physical capital is taken into account, the nation saved only 2 percent of its income last year, an unusually low level for the world's leading economy. At the same time, the nation's net domestic investment was 8 percent of its income. The difference, 6 percent of income, was financed by increases in net foreign claims on the United States and manifested itself in the current-account deficit.

Economists generally agree that the nation's current-account deficit cannot be sustained indefinitely at its current level relative to gross domestic product (GDP) because the nation's indebtedness to the rest of the world will grow faster than its income. Moreover, foreign investors will not continue to be willing to purchase U.S. claims at current rates of return indefinitely as their portfolios become more and more concentrated in such assets. To be sure, views differ on whether a future adjustment in the current-account deficit will occur gradually or suddenly—but there is little disagreement that some sort of adjustment is inevitable.

The necessary adjustment of the current-account deficit, which requires slower growth of consumption in the future, could take place slowly or rapidly. The more likely scenario appears to be a gradual adjustment without severe short-term economic consequences, but a sudden adjustment remains a risk—and possibly a growing risk as foreign net holdings of claims on the United States rise as a percentage of GDP. Policymakers can help facilitate the necessary reduction in the current- account deficit and reduce the risk of a severe economic disruption in foreign financing by taking actions to raise the rate of national saving.

ESTIMATED HOLDINGS OF U.S. GOVERNMENT SECURITIES BY FOREIGN INVESTORS

Foreign holdings of U.S. Treasury securities have grown rapidly in recent years. In 2003, for example, U.S. Treasury securities held by foreign investors amounted to $1.45 trillion, and by 2006, those holdings rose to $2.13 trillion—an increase of 47 percent.[1] As a percentage of total Treasury debt held by the public, foreign holdings rose from 37 percent to 44 percent over that span.[2] The increase in foreign holdings accounted for about 86 percent of total federal borrowing last year and about 72 percent from 2003 to 2006.

According to survey estimates, East Asian countries held a large share of foreign holdings of Treasury securities last year—about 63 percent.[3] The two East Asian countries with the largest holdings were Japan, which held an estimated 31 percent of all foreign-held Treasury securities, and mainland China, with 19 percent. In comparison, the European Union held an estimated 15 percent, and oil-exporting countries in the Middle East, about 5 percent.

Foreign official institutions have played a significant role in the increase in foreign ownership of federal debt. Indeed, at the end of 2006, foreign central banks owned 66 percent of all federal debt held by foreign residents, up from 63 percent at the end of 2005.

The data on ownership by country and by type of foreign entity (official versus private) are imperfect.[4] The surveys used to collect the data do not always capture the ultimate owner of the securities. If an owner entrusts securities with a custodian in a different country, for example, the ownership of the securities is attributed to the country of the custodian, not the owner. That "custodial bias" contributes to the large recorded foreign holdings of U.S. securities in major financial centers such as Belgium, the Caribbean banking centers, Luxembourg, Switzerland, and the United Kingdom.[5] Similarly, some foreign official purchases may be misclassified as foreign private ones because they are conducted through private-sector traders.

Foreign investors also hold a growing share of securities of U.S. agencies and government-sponsored enterprises (GSEs), evidently reflecting a drive to increase the returns on their investments. At the end of 2006, those investors owned about $1.2 trillion of such securities, more than twice as much as in 2001. The countries with the largest holdings were China, with about 23 percent of all such foreign holdings, and Japan, with about 17 percent.

Examining only the securities of the Treasury Department and of agencies and the GSEs that are held by foreign investors, however, obscures the broader and more fundamental issue: the rising net foreign claims on the United States that result from the nation's current-account deficit. The specific distribution of those foreign claims among different types of assets (U.S. government debt, equities, real estate, and so forth) may be important for considering some questions (for example, the potential for short-term disruptions in specific financial markets), but the overall level of those claims is more important in weighing other issues (for example, the vulnerability of the U.S. economy to adverse economic shocks). It is therefore important to emphasize that Treasury and other agency debt held by foreign investors represents only a portion of the total claims on the United States owned by the rest of the world.

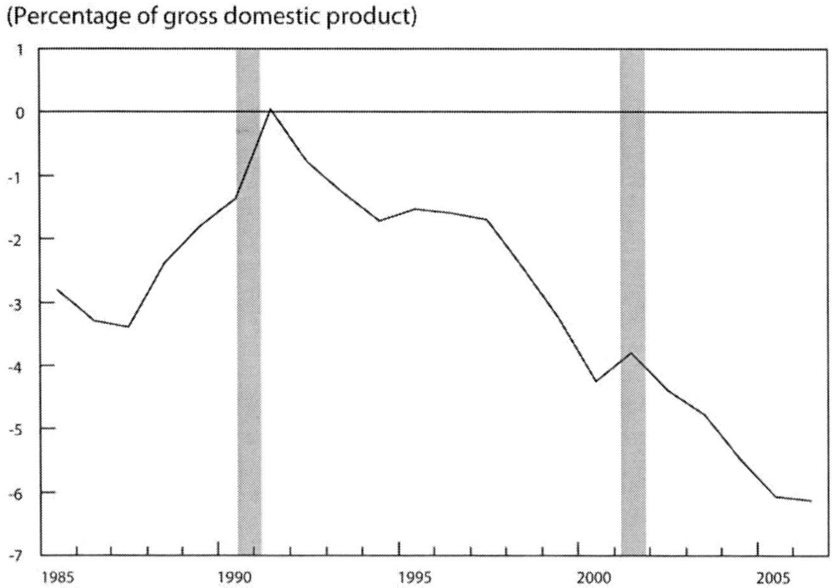

Sources: Congressional Budget Office; Department of Commerce, Bureau of Economic Analysis.

Note: Data are annual.

Figure 1. U.S. Current-Account Balance.

According to the Bureau of Economic Analysis, the total amount of claims on the United States held by foreign investors in 2005 amounted to $13.6 trillion—9 percent more than in 2004 and 52 percent more than in 2000. A little more than 17 percent in 2005 was U.S. government securities, up from about 13 percent in 2000 (see Table 1). As noted, much of the rise in the share of U.S. government securities was associated with increased holdings by foreign governments, rather than by foreign private investors. The key point, though, is that however the claims are allocated among different asset types and foreign owners, the broader issue is the overall rise in net foreign claims on the United States assets; that rise is necessary to finance the nation's current-account deficit.

THE FALL IN THE U.S. CURRENT-ACCOUNT BALANCE

The current-account balance fell from -1.7 percent of GDP in 1997 to a record -6.1 percent last year (see Figure 1 on page 5). At the same time, the outstanding amount of net international assets (holdings of claims on foreign entities by U.S. investors minus holdings of claims on the United States by foreign investors) fell from about -10 percent of GDP to about -20 percent in 2005 (see Figure 2).

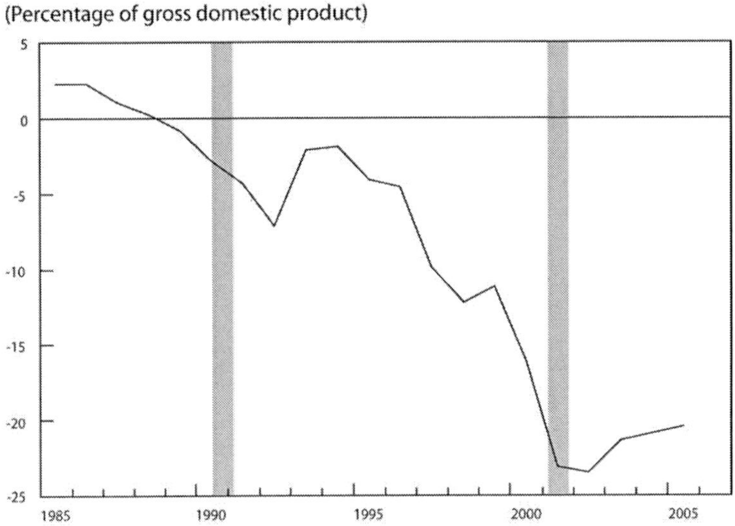

Sources: Congressional Budget Office; Department of Commerce, Bureau of Economic Analysis.

Notes:The market-value method values the owners' equity share of direct investment using indexes of stock market prices.

Data are annual. Data for 2006 are scheduled to be released on June 28, 2007.

Figure 2. Market Value of Net International Assets.

To examine why the deficit in the current-account balance has increased in recent years, it is useful to examine trends in both net domestic investment and net national saving.[6] Net domestic investment climbed steadily throughout the 1990s and then declined, on balance, in the early 2000s. On average, it has been 7 percent of national income since 1990 and in the past four years (see Figure 3).

Table 1. U.S. Assets and Liabilities Held by Foreign Investors, Selected Years, 1982 to 2005

	1982	1992	2000	2001	2002	2003	2004	2005
Total								
In trillions of dollars	0.7	2.9	9.0	9.3	9.3	10.7	12.5	13.6
As a percentage of U.S. GDP	22.3	46.1	91.5	91.5	88.5	97.2	106.9	109.4
Distribution (Percent)								
Total	100.0	100.0	100.0	100.0	100.0	100.0	100.0	100.0
Owned by foreign governments	26.1	15.0	11.5	12.0	13.5	14.7	16.0	16.3
Owned by foreign private sector	73.9	85.0	88.5	88.0	86.5	85.3	84.0	83.7
U.S. Government	23.7	18.8	12.9	13.4	15.8	16.2	16.6	17.4
Owned by foreign governments	20.2	12.0	8.6	9.3	10.7	11.3	12.1	12.2
Owned by foreign private sector	3.6	6.8	4.2	4.0	5.1	4.9	4.5	5.2
U.S. Private Sector	76.3	81.2	87.1	86.6	84.2	83.8	83.4	82.6
Direct investment[a]	18.0	23.9	31.0	27.6	21.8	23.0	21.6	20.5
Stocks (by private foreigners)	10.5	10.3	17.3	15.9	13.5	16.1	15.7	15.5
Bonds (by private foreigners)	2.3	10.3	11.9	14.5	16.5	16.1	16.2	16.7
Stocks and bonds (by foreign governments)	2.5	1.1	1.1	1.2	1.2	1.5	1.7	1.9
Liabilities of U.S. banks	34.9	24.2	14.7	15.8	18.3	19.9	21.5	21.2
U.S. currency	4.3	3.9	2.8	3.0	3.3	3.0	2.7	2.6
Other	3.8	7.5	8.3	8.6	9.6	4.2	4.0	4.2

Sources: Congressional Budget Office; Department of Commerce, Bureau of Economic Analysis.

Notes: GDP = gross domestic product.

Distribution shares are measured by market value.

a. Foreign direct investment in the United States is a foreign entity's ownership or control of 10 percent or more of the voting shares of a U.S. corporation.

Net domestic investment can be financed either by net national saving or net foreign claims on U.S. assets. Since the late 1990s, it has been financed more and more by foreign claims, as the rate of net national saving has declined from an average of 4-½ percent in the 1990s to an average of 1 percent in the past four years. From that perspective, the low level of national saving has been responsible for the elevated level of the current-account deficit.

The decline in the rate of national saving in the 2000s largely reflects movements in both federal and private net saving rates (see Figure 4). The decline in the federal net saving rate from 2000 to 2003 accounts for much of the decline in the net national saving rate over that period. After 2003, however, the rate of net federal saving rose, but the net national saving rate was little changed because the net private saving rate fell. Although federal saving and national saving do not move in lockstep, there is generally a close relationship between changes in federal saving and changes in national saving. Put simply, the more the federal government saves, the more the nation tends to save as a whole.

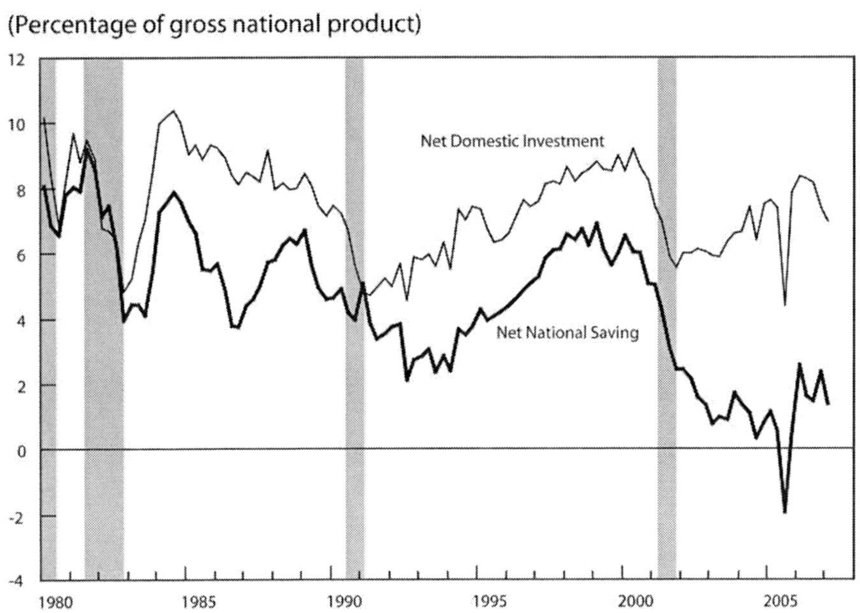

Sources: Congressional Budget Office; Department of Commerce, Bureau of Economic Analysis.

Notes: The sharp declines in 2005 reflect the capital losses from hurricanes, particularly Hurricane Katrina.

Data are quarterly and are plotted through the first quarter of 2007.

Figure 3. Net National Saving and Net Domestic Investment.

From another perspective, the elevated level of the nation's current-account deficit has been driven by the willingness of foreign investors to provide capital to the United States. In other words, the nation's rate of domestic investment is possible, given the rate of domestic saving, only because foreign entities have been willing to invest significant sums in U.S. assets and securities. From this perspective, inflows of capital from abroad affect the current account by raising the exchange value of the dollar and asset prices in the United States. The strong dollar encourages purchases of imports by U.S. residents and discourages purchases of U.S. exports by the rest of the world. Higher asset prices and correspondingly lower interest rates encourage consumption and investment.

Sources: Congressional Budget Office; Department of Commerce, Bureau of Economic Analysis.

Note: Data are quarterly and are plotted through the first quarter of 2007.

Figure 4. Net National, Private, and Federal Saving.

Table 2. Private and Official Financing of the U.S. Current-Account Deficit, 1990 to 2006

(Billions of U.S. dollars)									
	Annual Average								
	1990-1996	**1997-1999**	**2000**	**2001**	**2002**	**2003**	**2004**	**2005**	**2006**
Current-Account Deficit	82	219	417	385	460	522	640	755	811
plus									
Statistical Discrepancy and Other Net Inflows[a]	9	-43	69	16	44	17	-83	23	22
equals									
Total Net Capital Inflows	91	176	486	400	503	539	557	777	833
Net private inflows	27	160	445	378	391	259	154	498	385
Direct investment[b]	-21	34	162	25	-70	-86	-133	117	-55
Portfolio investment[c]	47	126	283	353	461	345	288	382	440
Net official inflows[d]	64	15	42	23	113	280	402	279	448

Sources: Congressional Budget Office; Department of Commerce, Bureau of Economic Analysis.

Note: Negative numbers denote capital outflows.

a. Other net inflows consist mainly of debt forgiveness and transfers by migrants to their home countries. Such inflows are small relative to the statistical discrepancy. A statistical discrepancy could stem from many factors, such as timing differences between the recording of trade flows (exports and imports) and the recording of the capital flows corresponding to those trade flows, inaccurate valuation, incomplete reporting, and errors from estimating procedures.

b. Direct-investment inflows are increases in foreign direct-investment assets in the United States, which are a foreign entity's ownership or control of 10 percent or more of the voting shares of a U.S. corporation. Direct-investment outflows are defined analogously.

c. Portfolio-investment inflows are increases in foreign holdings of U.S. stocks, bonds (including Treasury securities), U.S. currency, and other claims on U.S. banks, corporations, and individuals. Portfolio-investment outflows are increases in U.S. holdings of foreign stocks, bonds, and other claims of U.S. entities on foreigners.

d. Official inflows are increases in foreign governments' holdings of assets in the United States. Official outflows are increases in the U.S. government's holdings of assets abroad.

The willingness of foreign investors to buy U.S. debts and assets reflects the attractiveness of the United States as a destination for international investment because of its stable political environment, developed legal institutions, deep and liquid capital market, and strong banking and financial system, among other advantages. Moreover, because the U.S. dollar is the major medium of international transactions, it is less susceptible to extreme and sudden depreciation.[7] Indeed, the longevity of the large U.S. current-account deficit can be viewed as reflecting a sequence of events that caused demand for U.S. assets to grow even faster than the supply. Between 1997 and 2000, a host of developments—financial globalization, a succession of financial crises (the 1997–1998 Asian crisis, Russia's default of 1998, and the Brazilian *real* crisis of 1999), and weaker economic growth in other industrial countries than in the United States—all added to the demand for U.S. assets.[8] By propelling the dollar and U.S. asset prices higher, those developments contributed to widening the current-account deficit.

A significant share of the nation's overall external financing has been from foreign governments in recent years, as suggested by the trends in foreign ownership of U.S. government debt (see Table 2). In 2006, for example, net official inflows (purchases of claims on the United States by foreign governments net of purchases of claims on foreign entities by the U.S. government) were $448 billion, more than half of the $811 billion current-account deficit. Net official inflows also have grown rapidly in the past few years; in 2000, for example, net official inflows were only $42 billion. Almost all official purchases of U.S. assets were made by a handful of Asian governments, particularly China, which did so in order to keep its currency from appreciating outside of the band specified by its managed exchange rate policy. The Japanese government was also actively making purchases to keep the yen from rising before the spring of 2004.

THE UNSUSTAINABILITY OF THE CURRENT-ACCOUNT DEFICIT

Regardless of whether its financing is provided by foreign governments or foreign private investors, the large U.S. current-account deficit, analysts generally agree, cannot be sustained indefinitely at its present high level relative to GDP. The United States—like any other country—cannot continue accumulating debt at a rate faster than its ability to repay it. If policy actions or other economic developments do not reduce the current-account deficit, at some point foreign investors will become less willing to keep adding to their holdings of U.S. assets.

To be sure, net U.S. international assets have changed little relative to GDP in recent years despite the large current-account deficit, but that situation is unlikely to continue over the long run. Movements in asset prices and in the exchange rate have raised the dollar value of U.S.-owned foreign securities and direct investments overseas by more than that of U.S. securities and investments held by foreign investors, offsetting the consequence of the current-account deficit. However, such favorable effects of valuation cannot be relied on in the long term, and sooner or later net U.S. international assets will begin to fall rapidly relative to GDP if the large U.S. current-account deficit persists.

A persistently large current-account deficit will, over time, make foreign investors less willing to provide low-cost financing for it. To date, foreign demand for dollar assets has not yet weakened significantly, in part because the dollar is still the major international reserve currency. However, once investors accumulate enough dollar assets to facilitate international transactions and to meet their other needs for holding reserves, they are likely to slow down their purchases of dollar assets for those purposes and increasingly will buy or sell dollar assets on the basis of the expected returns. For example, the Chinese government announced in March this year that it would establish an investment agency to more "profitably" and "efficiently" manage a portion of its foreign reserves, which exceeded $1.2 trillion in the first quarter of this year.[9] Thus, to the extent that investors and governments believe that the U.S. current-account deficit will cause the dollar to depreciate, which reduces the expected return on dollar assets, the demand for dollar assets will fall.

Once foreign demand for U.S. assets begins to grow more slowly than the supply, there will be growing downward pressure on the dollar and U.S. asset prices. A lower dollar raises the prices of imports and reduces U.S. residents' purchasing power at home and abroad, and lower asset prices make U.S. residents poorer. As a result, U.S. residents will be less able and willing to borrow and spend, thereby lowering the current-account deficit; the exchange rate and asset price adjustments, in other words, will facilitate the reduction in the current-account deficit. As long as foreign demand for dollar assets does not drop too suddenly, the adjustment in the current account will be a gradual one. In that case, growth of the U.S. economy is likely to remain on track. The gradual rise in exports and decline in imports will entail more production and employment in sectors that export and sectors that compete with imports, helping to offset the negative effects of the gradual adjustment in asset prices, interest rates, and the prices of imports.

How bumpy the adjustment of the U.S. current account will be thus depends on what happens to foreign demand for U.S. assets. If short-term factors boost the growth in the demand for U.S. assets above the growth in supply, the U.S. current-account deficit may temporarily widen further. However, it seems implausible that foreign demand for U.S. assets will be boosted repeatedly by short-term factors. Once long-term downward pressures on demand begin to outweigh temporary supports for dollar assets, they will push down the dollar and those asset prices, facilitating the decline of the current-account deficit.[10]

Various factors may mitigate the risk of the type of sudden collapse in foreign financing that would be associated with a relatively rapid adjustment of the current account. For example, the unique role of the U.S. dollar as the world's main reserve currency should help to reduce the probability of a sudden stop of foreign financing, at least in the near future (although some analysts have warned that the dollar's role as a primary reserve currency cannot be taken for granted over the long run). Furthermore, nearly all U.S. international liabilities are denominated in dollars, and about two-thirds of U.S. holdings of assets abroad are equity assets, denominated in host countries' currencies. Therefore, a large depreciation of the dollar would lower net U.S. liabilities to foreign investors not only by lowering net imports but also by boosting the dollar value of U.S. assets abroad. Consequently, the depreciation would not necessarily feed on itself and become a full-blown dollar crisis, unlike the effects of a sharp drop in the currency of a country with a large amount of debt denominated in foreign currencies.[11]

Thus, the more likely scenario appears to be a gradual adjustment, in which the current account falls gradually over time.[12] Nonetheless, given the likelihood of a continued decline in the United States' net international assets as a percentage of GDP, a risk remains that adjustments in the foreign exchange rate and the current account will occur more rapidly than anticipated and that the effects of a rapid adjustment on the economy will be much more severe than with a gradual adjustment. That risk probably increases as the nation's net international assets fall as a percentage of GDP.

POLICY OPTIONS

Policymakers cannot directly control the current-account deficit, but they can influence the factors that determine it. Because the current account is equal to the difference between national saving and investment in the United States, policies that influence saving or investment will affect it. Although the current-account deficit could be improved by reducing investment, that outcome would be undesirable. With less investment, the U.S. capital stock would grow more slowly, which would reduce the growth of productivity and real wages over time. Therefore, the more desirable options for reducing the current-account deficit are those that would raise national saving.

Focusing on national saving may be particularly important in light of the economic and budgetary outlook in the United States over the next several decades. Rising federal health care costs, in particular, will place mounting pressure on federal spending, and if revenues remain at their current shares of GDP, the federal budget deficit is projected to grow rapidly, which could substantially reduce national saving.[13] Over the past four decades, Medicare's and Medicaid's costs per beneficiary have increased about 2.5 percentage points faster per year than has per capita GDP. If those costs continued growing at the same rate over the next four decades, federal spending on those two programs alone would rise from 4.5 percent of GDP today to about 20 percent by 2050 (see Figure 5). Indeed, the rate at which health care costs grow relative to income is the most important determinant of the long-term fiscal balance; it exerts a significantly larger influence on the budget over the long term than other commonly cited factors, such as the aging of the population.[14]

National saving can be increased in a number of ways that could involve higher government saving and/or higher private saving. Raising government saving through deficit reduction is one of the most reliable ways through which policymakers could boost national saving. That goal could be achieved through higher taxes, lower spending, or both.[15] Given the nature of the nation's long-term fiscal challenge, controlling the growth of federal health care costs seems a key component of deficit reduction over the next several decades. A variety of evidence suggests that opportunities exist to constrain health care costs both in the public programs and in the overall health care system without adverse health consequences, although capturing those opportunities to reduce costs without harming health outcomes involves many challenges.

National saving could also be increased through higher private saving. In evaluating policies to raise private saving, it is important to include their effects on government saving. For example, general tax incentives for private saving financed through higher budget deficits might not generate enough additional private saving to offset the higher budget deficits. Consequently, even if such policies increased private saving, they might not raise national saving. By contrast, deficit-neutral policies that encouraged private saving would work to raise national saving (because the increase in private saving would not be offset by a reduction in government saving).

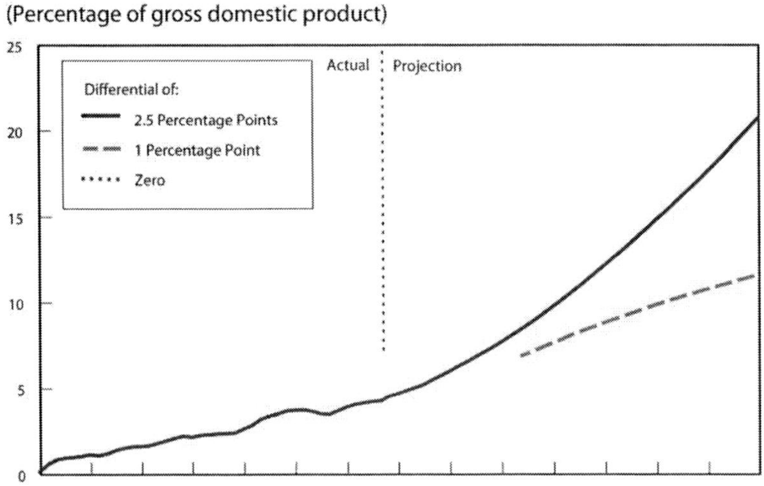

Source: Congressional Budget Office.

Note: The health cost growth differential refers to the number of percentage points by which the growth of annual health care spending per beneficiary is assumed to exceed the growth of nominal gross domestic product per capita, after an adjustment for the growth and aging of the Medicare and Medicaid populations.

Figure 5. Total Federal Spending for Medicare and Medicaid Under Assumptions About the Health Cost Growth Differential.

Various options for raising private saving in such a manner have been proposed—for example, establishing automatic aspects for 401(k) and similar savings plans. Currently, many such plans leave it up to the employee to choose whether to participate, how much to contribute, which investment vehicle offered by the employer to select, and when to pull the funds out of the plan and in what form. Workers are thus confronted with a series of financial decisions, each of which involves risk and a certain degree of financial expertise. Many workers shy away from those decisions and simply do not make them, and the result is often a lack of participation. Research has suggested that participation and contribution levels can be substantially affected by changing the defaults at each of those points of decision. Indeed, one of the strongest empirical findings from behavioral economics is that automatic enrollment—that is, enrolling workers in a plan unless they opt out, as opposed to requiring them to sign up in order to participate—boosts the rate of participation substantially.[16] Legislation enacted last year makes it easier for corporations to offer 401(k)-type plans with automatic enrollment and other automatic features, and researchers have proposed ways of expanding the same logic to individual retirement accounts.[17] If such proposals were financed in a deficitneutral anner, so that any gains to private saving were not offset by decreases in government saving, they could increase national saving. However, even if they were implemented in that manner, they would probably generate only a fraction of the saving needed to close the current-account deficit.

However it is accomplished, achieving a higher level of national saving also entails drawbacks. In the end, policies that raise national saving have one thing in common: They reduce consumption of goods and services and/or leisure. What makes the policies different is how they affect specific households and how they affect the economy at large. Therefore, choosing the appropriate saving policy inevitably involves balancing the economic effects of alternative policies with their distributional consequences.

Despite those various trade-offs and however it is accomplished, encouraging higher national saving probably represents the most effective step that policymakers can take to facilitate the necessary reduction in the current-account deficit and reduce the risk of a severe economic disruption in foreign financing.

End Notes

[1] *Budget of the United States Government, Fiscal Year 2008: Analytical Perspectives*, p. 235.

[2] Although not strictly comparable, the percentage of federal debt held by foreign investors was estimated to be 32 percent in 1997 and 15 percent in 1985.

[3] Department of the Treasury, Federal Reserve Bank of New York, and Board of Governors of the Federal Reserve System, *Report on Foreign Portfolio Holdings of U.S. Securities, as of June 30, 2006* (May 2007).

[4] See Department of the *Treasury, Frequently Asked Questions Regarding the TIC System and TIC Data*, available at www.ustreas.gov/tic/faq1.shtml.

[5] Ibid.

[6] Those net measures account for depreciation of the existing capital stock.

[7] The dollar's status as the major reserve currency has meant that foreign demand for dollar assets has increased as other economies and international transactions have grown.

[8] Financial globalization has allowed private foreign investors to participate in the U.S. capital market more fully. See Congressional Budget Office, *The Decline in the U.S. Current-Account Balance Since 1991* (August 6, 2004).

[9] The announcement did not specify how much of the reserves would be managed initially by the new agency, but Chinese officials and the press have suggested an amount of up to $300 billion.

[10] The trade-weighted dollar exchange rate relative to currencies in major industrial countries, computed by the Federal Reserve Board, declined about 9 percent between November 2005 and May 2007.

[11] For such an indebted country, its currency's depreciation necessarily raises the domestic-currency values of its international debt and interest payments on that debt but may not have a significant effect on the value of its trade surplus (especially if its exports rely significantly on imported materials). Thus, its net debt could become higher even as its currency depreciates, putting greater downward pressure on its currency.

[12] See Congressional Budget Office, *Will the U.S. Current Account Have a Hard or Soft Landing?* (June 11, 2007).

[13] See Congressional Budget Office, *The Long-Term Budget Outlook* (December 2005).

[14] See Statement of Peter R. Orszag, Director, Congressional Budget Office, *Health Care and the Budget: Issues and Challenges for Reform*, before the Senate Committee on the Budget (June 21, 2007).

[15] In evaluating alternative ways to reduce the budget deficit, it is important to be mindful of the potential effects of those policies on private saving. Some policies could reduce private saving. However, although the impact would depend on the nature of the policy change, reductions in private saving, if they occurred, would probably not be large enough to completely offset the gains to national saving from lower budget deficits.

[16] See, for example, Brigitte Madrian and Dennis Shea, "The Power of Suggestion: Inertia in 401(k) Participation and Savings Behavior," *Quarterly Journal of Economics,* vol. 116, no. 4 (November 2001), p. 1160.

[17] See J. Mark Iwry and David John, *Pursuing Universal Retirement Security Through Automatic IRAs* (Washington, D.C.: Retirement Security Project, February 2006).

INDEX

A

B

C

D

E

F

S

T

U

V

W